Toward a Holistic Intelligence

Toward a Holistic Intelligence

Life on the Other Side of the Digital Barrier

Lyn Lesch

ROWMAN & LITTLEFIELD
Lanham • Boulder • New York • London

Published by Rowman & Littlefield
An imprint of The Rowman & Littlefield Publishing Group, Inc.
4501 Forbes Boulevard, Suite 200, Lanham, Maryland 20706
www.rowman.com

86-90 Paul Street, London EC2A 4NE, United Kingdom

British Library Cataloguing in Publication Information Available

Library of Congress Cataloging-in-Publication Data Available

Names: Lesch, Lyn, 1948– author.
Title: Toward a holistic intelligence : life on the other side of the digital
    barrier / Lyn Lesch.
Description: Lanham : Rowman & Littlefield, 2022. | Includes
    bibliographical references. | Summary: "Beginning with an
    examination of how our current digital age is negatively affecting
    our cognitive lives and overall intelligence, Toward a Holistic
    Intelligence then explores how an intelligence based on direct
    insight, one which germinates from our sensorial and emotive lives,
    might provide a possible solution"— Provided by publisher.
Identifiers: LCCN 2021041204 (print) | LCCN 2021041205 (ebook) |
    ISBN 9781475863734 (cloth) | ISBN 9781475863741
    (paperback) | ISBN 9781475863758 (epub)
Subjects: LCSH: Information society—Psychological aspects. | Internet
    users—Psychology. | Intellect. | Cognition.
Classification: LCC HM851 .L4648 2022 (print) | LCC HM851
    (ebook) | DDC 303.48/33—dc23
LC record available at https://lccn.loc.gov/2021041204
LC ebook record available at https://lccn.loc.gov/2021041205

To all those who never stop searching

Contents

Preface

Significant truths about various areas of human endeavor often approach us indirectly out of the corner of our eye, only to be found with the greatest degree of discerning thought. Possibly this is so due to their essential nature, that they speak of a larger reality that is often hidden from human awareness; a reality that has become not so obvious simply because it is so important, and so requires the most serious creative investigation to apprehend it.

Such may well be the case in terms of how the present digital age, with all of its incredible tools, may be negatively affecting human consciousness, and how the search for some larger form of intelligence may be what is now desperately needed; one in which our mental lives can't possibly be abrogated by the effects of the digital world due to the nature of this larger intelligence; that it exists beyond the reach of those potentially deleterious effects in a larger world beyond them.

It has already been well documented how our obsessive use of digital devices in our current Internet age is impeding our working memories and our attention spans, as well as consistently interrupting the stream of our thoughts. Yet at the same time what seems to have been left significantly unaddressed relative to these adverse effects is how they may be preventing us from being more in touch with the sort of larger consciousness which necessarily requires the sort of subtle, indirect intelligence alluded to above.

If we are not fully in touch with the illusory nature of both memory and thought, we may well never be able to find a comfortable place on the other side of them, one in which both intuition and direct insight become the new benchmarks for a larger intelligence; and to be fully in touch with the dynamics inherent in thought and memory would seem to necessarily require seeing them both with the greatest degree of clarity.

It may well be true that our greatest purpose as human beings inhabiting this small planet spinning in space is to seek a consciousness which points toward a limitless reality, one which exists beyond the boundaries of the self, thought, knowledge, and the past in search of some universal meaning.

At this point in time, it would appear to be true that if we are ever to seek that larger consciousness, we may need to find the most intelligent way to approach it. Therefore, that is exactly what this book is about; the possibility that by seeking to combine our emotive, sensorial, and intuitive lives into a larger awareness born of direct insight, one which might yet transcend the potentially negative effects on thought and memory which our current digital age has brought, we may yet be able to put ourselves in touch with a holistic intelligence leading toward a larger, potentially limitless consciousness; one which may well be our potential birthright as human beings.

Acknowledgments

I am grateful to my editor at Rowman & Littlefield, Tom Koerner, who was willing to publish this book and my previous book, *Intelligence in the Digital Age: How the Search for Something Larger May Be Imperiled,* two offbeat books whose subject matter, although critically important, does not yet fully exist in the modern world. I am also grateful to Jim Wasner, Bill Pollack, and Renee and Dave Porter for the numerous discussions I have had with them over the years concerning topics which are relative to these books, discussions which have helped to sharpen my focus in writing them. I am likewise grateful to my sister-in-law Sheryl Lesch, whose enthusiasm for and support of both my writing and my life have always meant so much to me. Above all, I am grateful to my brother Chip Lesch, who gave me constant support and encouragement to pursue this project, as well as the previous one, and who provided me with any number of books and articles for research purposes, as well as ideas. Without his continued assistance and support, both this book and the previous one might never have come to fruition.

Introduction

In 2020 I published *Intelligence in the Digital Age: How the Search for Something Larger May Be Imperiled*; a book that examined how our current Internet age and people's increasing use of digital devices may be affecting both their mental capacities and emotive lives in ways that make it increasingly difficult for those of us who are interested in doing so to explore the possibility of a larger, more expansive consciousness.

That is, because the natural stream of our thoughts, our attention spans, our working memories, and the depth of our emotive lives are being potentially abrogated by people's addictive use of their smartphones and PCs, these same personal dynamics which are so necessary for an examination of the limits of our thinking minds in search of a larger awareness, simply because they are now being stifled, are inevitably going to make that exploration of a larger consciousness significantly more difficult.

As the increasing number of those who have studied the matter thoroughly are most likely already aware, the appearance of the Internet, and people's continuous use of digital devices, has had profound effects on both their mental and emotive lives. Yet to date, this discussion has seemingly only involved ways in which we might somehow either alter our use of digital technologies or else change our apprehension of them so that those negative dynamics don't continue to occur.

Yet it would appear, with all due respect to those who have studied the effects of our habitual devices upon all of us, so far the discussion seems to have centered upon how we might either limit our use of such devices in a manner which might potentially minimize their potential deleterious effects upon all of us, or simply make people, particularly those young people who have never known a world which didn't include the Internet, more aware of exactly what those negative effects are and how they might occur.

In other words, how our current digital age may be adversely affecting our cognitive lives, memories, and emotive lives has not yet involved a discussion of how we might overcome these potentially adverse effects by seeking a larger intelligence which in fact exists on the other side of thought and memory; one which is anchored in an enriched sensorial and emotive life that our continuous use of digital technologies won't be able to substantially affect. In addition, such a larger intelligence might likewise lead toward a more expansive consciousness that could substantially enrich our inner lives, as well as sharpen our awareness.

To this end, this book should serve as an exploratory jumping off point for a consideration of what that larger intelligence might specifically entail, and how we might begin to facilitate it within ourselves. Although it is by no means a final definitive statement concerning the potential exploration of a holistic, integrated intelligence which might exist beyond our rational thoughts and working memories, and so should be taken in that spirit, still it will hopefully provoke discussion of the issue, both in terms of the potentially negative effects on us of our current Internet age, and likewise in terms of a more expansive view of the meaning of intelligence.

No doubt, there will be scientists, philosophers, educators, and others who may take issue with some of the statements here which they believe to be unprovable, at least in the present moment. However, what those experts may do well to consider is that many of the ideas explored here, because they exist in a world that is often beyond the bounds of thought, memory, and previous knowledge, should be considered as part of a larger, more expansive vision that does not yet fully exist in the modern world.

Yet at the same time it seems relatively certain that both the Internet and how we are using our digital devices are affecting us profoundly. Consequently, if the effects on our thinking minds, attention spans, working memories, and emotive lives are indeed as adverse as they might appear to be, there would seem to be two approaches we might take in endeavoring to counteract this potential development.

Either we can somehow try to limit the extent to which we use the exciting but potentially hazardous devices which have in fact become our new reality, or we can seek to explore the possibility of the growth of an intelligence that is beyond the reach of the Internet and all its resulting technologies, one that is fundamentally anchored in our sensorial and emotive lives. The first, it would seem might not be realistic simply because the digital world has now become so thoroughly embedded in all our lives.

The second, however, although being part of a serious exploration into the unknown, might potentially allow us to develop an expansive awareness that the Internet and digital age won't be able to negatively affect, while at the same time, that larger awareness might in fact lead toward the sort of holistic intelligence existing beyond the bounds of thought, memory, and even knowledge which philosophers, thinkers, and others have sought for as long as people have raised serious questions about the nature and meaning of our existence in this world; a place which the digital technologies we have recently developed might not be able to reach.

Chapter 1

A Holistic Intelligence

Throughout human history, people have invariably made sense of the details of their world primarily through the use of rational thought and memory; using the former to think about what their experiences may be telling them, and the latter to recall important aspects of their experience which might lead them to the truths concerning it. That is, it has generally been assumed that without the power of rational thought, that which is based largely upon memory, one will be left with an unfocused apprehension of what his experience may be telling him; and will therefore be left adrift in negotiating the complexities of his immediate environment.

At the same time, the concept of intelligence has remained significantly tethered to the idea of cognitive ability. In general layman's terms, when one imagines what it is to be an intelligent person, one invariably thinks of one's capacity to reason clearly and efficiently, or else considers the amount of knowledge about the world which a person has been able to store in their long-term memory during the course of their life.

Recently, two well received works by researchers attempted to frame the concept of intelligent apprehension of one's world within a broader context. In his classic 1995 bestselling book *Emotional Intelligence,* Daniel Goleman put forth the idea that humans have what he refers to as "two minds," the rational and emotional, with the latter including such qualities as self-awareness, self-discipline, and empathy.

Similarly, Harvard professor Howard Gardner, in his popular 1983 book *Frames of Mind: The Theory of Multiple Intelligences,* made the argument that people possess a number of different types of intelligence, such as visual-spatial, verbal-linguistic, bodily-kinesthetic, or

1

logical-mathematical; Gardner claiming that individual people differ in terms of how strong or dominant a certain type of intelligence is within them.

And yet, the exclusive idea of intelligent apprehension of one's world as being the product of rational thought has by and large continued to resonate with the general public, along with the notion that the amount of knowledge or information one has obtained as a result of their life experience is likewise of primary importance. We as humans continue to largely believe that the best way to form a clear picture of our world, one that will allow us to effectively make our way through it, is to use reason which is based upon memories of what has happened to us in the past.

Yet, as a result of the effects of our current digital age on people's attention spans and working memories, there is increasing evidence that the jumpy, fragmented awareness that is being inculcated in people by the great interruption machine that is the Internet is having a profound effect on the stream of people's thoughts and their capacity to follow those thoughts to a point of completion.

Likewise, the effects that the challenge of information overload brought about by the Internet is presenting to people's short-term memories, their capacity to turn those short-term memories into long-term ones, and the manner in which large search engines such as *Google* are in effect becoming our brain's external hard drive in significantly replacing our working memories are all having profoundly negative effects on our capacity to use our memories to clearly digest elements of ourselves and our world.

So the important questions here would appear to be: are we in effect dulling our capacities for rational thought and memory due to the potentially negative effects of the Internet on us, particularly due to people's increasingly obsessive use of their digital devices; and if this dulling process is potentially irreversible is there a new type of intelligence which might allow us to comprehend ourselves and our world more clearly, one that might exist beyond the bounds of rational thought and memory?

This of course brings up the idea of direct insight; the ability to immediately see the essence of a situation, person, idea, etc. by inhabiting a space beyond thought and memory. Some psychologists have referred to such a state as being in the *zone*. Others, such as noted

Hungarian psychologist Mihaly Csikszentmihalyi, have referred to such a place of immediate comprehension as a *flow state*; a place where the mind is able to make consistent connections between different areas of knowledge and information without any sort of interruptions or distractions preventing those connections from taking place.

If one believes that the power of direct insight has a significant place to play in allowing a person to clearly apprehend their world at a place beyond the activities of thought and memory, the question would appear to be one of how to facilitate such a state of mind. Consequently, certain questions related to the capacity for this type of immediate insight come rapidly to the fore.

How might our emotive and sensorial lives, in lieu of our cognitive life, become focal points for a new type of intelligence? How might our thoughts impede our emotive and sensorial reactions to our environment? What is the relationship between the stream of our thoughts and an intelligent apprehension of our world? How might moments of direct insight evolve from absorbing emotive or sensorial experience? And how do all these questions pertaining to an intelligence born of direct insight relate to one another?

Answers to these questions might involve emboldening both our emotive and sensorial lives in lieu of a predominately cognitive life, which means looking at the above questions and potential answers within a much larger context; at a place where the word *intelligence* might take on a much different meaning than that which has been formerly attributed to it.

Might it be that emotions and sensorial reactions are part of a larger intelligence which exists at a deeper level than most neuroscientists, psychologists, learning theorists, and others had previously imagined, one which exists beyond the bounds of thought and memory? And if so, might this larger intelligence become increasingly necessary due to the effects of the current digital age on our thoughts and memories?

These are obviously extremely complex questions, yet seemingly ones which might be successfully addressed if one is willing to adopt a more expansive view of what intelligence means, one which contains the idea that our emotive and sensorial lives might be able to exist at a deeper level than what we might have previously imagined; at a place where a larger intelligence born of direct insight begins to occur.

Likewise, it is almost certainly the power of direct insight which might allow one to perceive just how limiting the processes of thought and memory might be when they are not part of a larger absorption into the details and dynamics of one's world. That *aha* moment of creative absorption, as those who have examined the matter have discovered, can only truly come about when one is capable of seeing the essence of something in a *flash* because one is free of the energy-draining activities of thought and memory.

There is increasing evidence now that people's relentless use of their digital devices in this new age in which we now find ourselves is going to continue to both fragment and disrupt our thought processes as they become increasingly assimilated into the jumpy, fragmented nature of the interruption machine that is the Internet. That is, the once natural stream of our thoughts is being hijacked by the algorithms and coding inside our digital devices to mirror how they operate as we jump endlessly from link to link on our phones and PCs, with very little time left in between for fully assimilating whatever information we've just downloaded.

Nicholas Carr, in his prescient book *The Shallows: What the Internet Is Doing to Our Brains,* points to the fact that both the Internet and digital technologies are changing not just what we think, but the very process of thought itself, chipping away at our ability to attend by presenting information to us as a swiftly moving stream of particles which break our concentration into bits of unrelated knowledge.

Likewise, our memories are being continually dulled by information overload and by our use of large search engines as substitutes for our previous organic ways of recalling information and knowledge. In a very real sense, search engines such as *Google* are in effect becoming our brain's external hard drive as we relentlessly search for information and knowledge on them in lieu of following the networks of thought inside our minds to access what we might have forgotten.

Quite obviously, the Internet and the digital devices which it has spawned have now become the way that the world in fact works. In other words, both will only continue to become increasingly predominate in our lives. And most likely, so will their potential effects on our capacity to follow our thoughts to a point of completion and to use our working memories to recall significant information and knowledge.

What might be needed in response to this is a new way of seeing the details of our world clearly without depending so thoroughly on thought and memory; a more direct, insightful approach that is the function of a creative absorption into the world's details and dynamics. How that approach might be engendered will be explored in the pages which follow.

Chapter 2

Thought and Memory in the Digital Age

The Internet has often been described as a great interruption machine. As we jump from website to website, or immediately cease concentrating on what had been previously commanding our attention to open a text message, the previously continuous stream of our thoughts rapidly grows fragmented and jumpy. And over time, depending on how deeply engaged one is by their virtual devices, simply by force of habit one's own thought processes can easily become identical with that same jumpy, fragmented awareness.

Whether that type of digital habituation remains when one is not immediately engaged with one's mobile phone or PC is of course still an open-ended question; as is the question of whether Internet addiction is only psychological in nature, or does it originate on a more serious physiological level. Of course, if the latter is the case, that is if people are becoming actually physically addicted to their digital devices to the point where the addiction grows more permanent, even potentially irreversible where their brain chemistry is affected, then the problem is more deep seeded than if Internet addiction is only psychological in nature.

What would seem to be also true is that because the Internet tends to interrupt the stream of so many people's thoughts on such a regular basis, depending of course upon the amount of time they spend gazing into a plastic screen, that process of interruption is also going to have a significant effect on their capacity to use their power of reason to come to a clear apprehension of the particulars of their world. For how might someone effectively employ their ability to reason unless they are able to follow the stream of their thoughts to a point of completion?

Likewise, how could someone effectively follow the network of their thoughts that lead toward particular information and knowledge if they are regularly outsourcing their ability to do so to search engines such as *Google* in lieu of using organic networks which reside within their minds and brains to do so? It seems obvious that because those same neuronal networks are no longer being used to the same degree which they once were, then over time they will tend to dry up and calcify, leaving human memory stultified.

In addition, our ability to attend, to focus, is being similarly affected by how our short-term memories are consistently flooded by the Internet with more information than they can potentially absorb. Consequently, they become less able to pass that knowledge and information to our long-term memories, which allow us to focus, to decide exactly what we will pay attention to, and what we will not.

Our attention, if it is functioning properly, is very much a filter which allows us to decide which aspects of our immediate environment we will take in and process further so that both our senses and our thoughts don't grow overwhelmed by too many things coming at us all at once. When our minds are no longer able to properly filter out irrelevancies, everything comes at us too quickly, and as a result we can no longer properly attend to the dynamics and details of our world.

When we can no longer follow the stream of our thoughts to a point of completion, we lose the ability to think rationally. When we significantly lose the capacity to retrieve information and knowledge from the actual network of our thoughts, our memories grow increasingly dulled and dysfunctional. And when we can no longer properly attend to the details of our world because we have lost the ability to separate the relevant from the irrelevant, we lose our capacity to attend, to focus. When all three negative dynamics occur simultaneously, we lose the ability to think intelligently about ourselves and our world. Consequently, our perceptions of our immediate environment grow muddied and unclear.

Therefore, it would seem to be of the utmost importance in this new digital age which we have now entered that, due to the effects of the Internet on our thoughts, memories, and attention spans, that if we are no longer able to follow our thoughts to a point of completion, that if we are losing full access to our working memories, and that if our attention spans have grown distracted and diffuse, we may need to employ a different type of intelligence for apprehending our world.

Perhaps it is the case that both our emotions and the thoughts which follow from them possess a deeply embodied basis. That is, both might often originate in our physiological reactions to events in our lives. William James, the late nineteenth century philosopher, contrary to what had been thought to be true at the time, put forth the idea that our conscious experience of emotion actually tends to take place *after* the body's physical reaction to some event.

That is, when we encounter a potentially dangerous situation, such as suddenly meeting a bear in the woods, we do not first evaluate the degree of danger we might be in and then feel afraid. Instead, we first respond instinctively to the sight of the bear on a physiological level, for example through an increased heart rate, and then only later experience the conscious emotion of fear.

If such is indeed the case, then that might mean that both our thoughts and emotions might not only be more deeply connected to our physiological reactions to events in our lives than what we had previously imagined, but that the two of them might also be more deeply connected to each other in ways that we had not previously considered. This then would appear to create the further possibility that we might be able to better understand the relationship between thought and emotion at a significantly deeper level than what we had previously been able to do.

Psychologists such as Stanley Schachter at Columbia University in 1962 through a series of experiments involving both men and women in which he used the chemical epinephrine have been able to demonstrate that a person's emotional responses to events or situations are determined not only by their physiological responses to those events or situations, but also by the context in which they take place; meaning that the brain's interpretation of a particular physiological reaction to a specific situation is in fact a significant cause of a person's emotive reaction to it.

Thoughts, physical reactions, and emotions no doubt all have a highly complex relationship to one another, with one often influencing the others. Yet, as Nobel Prize-winning neuroscientist Eric Kandel asked in his prescient 2012 book *The Age of Insight: The Quest to Understand the Unconscious in Art, Mind, and Brain*, how are our emotional responses coordinated? What is the relationship between our feelings and the physiological changes triggered by emotionally charged stimuli? Furthermore, what exact role do our thoughts play in this whole process?

The answer to these questions no doubt might have a great deal to do with the development of an intelligence which originates in our emotive and sensorial reactions to the world at a place of direct insight and creative absorption; a place where the potential depth of those emotions and sensorial reactions can't be impeded by the potentially restrictive barriers of thought and memory. Naturally, such an intelligence might become critically important to engender if the Internet and people's obsessive use of their digital devices is affecting both the stream of their thoughts and their working memories in ways which prevent us from employing both rational thought and memory to comprehend our world as fully and effectively as we once did.

There is in fact a revealing scene about these matters in Jane Campion's mesmerizing movie *Bright Star*, which concerned the evolution of the intense love affair between the poet John Keats and his next-door neighbor the seamstress Fannie Brawne in early nineteenth-century England. During one of their lessons together in which Keats is teaching Brawne about the essence of poetry, he tells her that a poem needs to be understood through the senses. Using the example of someone diving into a lake, he reminds her that the point of diving into the lake is to be in the lake; to luxuriate in the sensation of water, not to work the lake out with one's thoughts.

David Bohm, the renowned twentieth-century physicist who contributed greatly to our understanding of quantum theory, particularly how subatomic particles existing at a distance from each other may be entangled, and who was also a close associate of Albert Einstein, wrote in his book *Wholeness and the Implicate Order* of how our experience of the world can become fragmented and unreal when it is based on our mistaking the content of our thoughts for our experience of the world as it is.

One of the things which Bohm was addressing was how words and thoughts by themselves can prevent us from perceiving our world more clearly simply because the word is never the thing itself, and because our system of thought and language has inherent limitations which can prevent us from not only discovering what is real, but likewise from perceiving the details and dynamics of our world within a more expansive context.

Bohm likewise addresses in his book the essential difference between *intelligence* and *thought;* referring to *thought* as a product of all of the conditioned responses of memory, while *intelligence* is an act of perception, rather than a process of thought, in which in a *flash* of understanding somebody is able to immediately perceive the actual irrelevance of their whole way of thinking about a certain problem, and instead apprehend it directly through a different approach in which all of the different elements of the problem fit in a new order and a new structure.

If one is in fact in agreement with Bohm on this issue, then a logical first step in integrating emotion and sensorial reactions into a larger intelligence, one born of direct insight and creative absorption, would be to explore the limitations of thought. Otherwise, it would seem, the thinking mind continues to be a barrier necessarily controlling and eventually limiting the sort of immediate perception of our world to which Bohm refers.

In likewise addressing the dynamic of immediate perception, one born of direct insight, the famous twentieth century philosopher and thinker Krishnamurti contrasted knowledge with intelligence; the former being something that is generated only through the assimilation of facts and information, while the latter is a process in which one is capable of seeing the essence of something in a *flash* exactly because one is free from the energy draining activities of thought.

Yet how could we possibly perceive and then understand the limitations of our thinking mind if our actual stream of thought is being continually fragmented and interrupted by the essential nature of the Internet, one which is increasingly making it extremely difficult, if not impossible, to follow our thoughts to a point of completion?

In a seminal study to be found in the May 2019 issue of *World Psychiatry,* user experience designer and experimental researcher Eyal Ophir and two colleagues were among the first to explore the sustained impact of media multitasking on cognitive capacities in a study of individuals who engaged in frequent and extensive multitasking compared to those who did not.

What the researchers found was that surprisingly those who were heavy multitaskers performed worse on tests that measured their ability to switch tasks while online than those who were not such consistent multitaskers. According to the researchers, closer inspection of this result suggested that the lesser ability to switch tasks shown by heavy multitasking individuals was due to their increased susceptibility to distraction from irrelevant stimuli.

This study, it would seem, appears to demonstrate that those who consistently use the Internet to multitask are less able to attend while switching tasks online even though it would seem logical to assume that their proficiency in this area might in fact be greater than those who did not use the Internet to multitask to a similar extent. What this might mean, of course, is that the sort of jumpy, fragmented awareness to which people are susceptible when they go online makes it even harder for Internet users to follow the stream of their thoughts from one site to another even though it might seem that their added practice in doing so might actually increase this capacity.

The study might likewise suggest, simply because the ability to think rationally about some significant piece of information or knowledge very much has to do with logically following the stream of one's thoughts through increasingly disparate areas of knowledge and information, that our capacity for rational thought might in fact now be in the process of being adversely affected by our online addictions.

The next question, of course, is whether such an interruption in the stream of one's thoughts might only take place when one is online, or if it can in fact become a regular part of one's psyche even if they are not using their cell phone, tablet, or PC. That is, can one's brain become permanently wired to engage in the same jumpy, interrupted awareness to which one is subjected when they go online to the point where it becomes increasingly difficult to think rationally simply because one has lost the capacity to follow the thread of one's thoughts?

Likewise, can one's working memory become permanently affected simply because one has continually outsourced the retrieval of facts and information to large search engines, and in the process deadened it through lack of use of the neuronal networks in one's brain that lead toward those facts and that information? Similarly, if one's short-term memory is continually subjected to information overload, and consequently the retrieval of information can't be as easily passed on to one's long-term memory, where it can be used to ferret out relevant from irrelevant information and knowledge, will one still be able to use both their working memory and their capacity to attend as effectively to think intelligently about oneself or one's world?

If the interruption machine that the Internet can often become is in fact causing us to apprehend our world less intelligently, then there would appear to be one of two choices facing us in this digital age of ours. Either we can attempt to prevent our use of digital technologies from impeding our thoughts and memories, or we can uncover new ways beyond thought and memory to apprehend our world, our selves, and our immediate environment.

Is there a direct insight stemming from a heightened awareness in which our interior life exists without any barriers—be they the result of either thought or memory—that separate us from the details of our world; one in which observer and observed become one and the same? This would mean a new type of intelligence which might on occasion be able to dispense with both rational thought and memory simply because it is capable of seeing the truth about something in an instant; through an immediate perception which requires neither logical thought nor memory of past experience or knowledge to maintain its clarity.

Furthermore, if such an insight were in fact possible, what would be the preconditions for its existence? One, according to those such as Krishnamurti, would be that someone is able to see the essence of something while possessed of an energy that sustains itself simply because their mind is free of the energy draining activities of thought. Another precondition, according to Professor of Psychology Mark Jung-Beeman of Northwestern University, would be a period of mental relaxation during which one is not encumbered by the activities of thought.

At the same time, for a true insight to take place, both one's sensorial and one's emotive life must likewise be able to exist at a level where there are no barriers separating one from the details of the world which he or she inhabits. Once again, a pure state of heightened physical perception in which the observer and the observed become one at a place where one's senses and emotions become fully energized.

Yet it is hard to see how that can occur if one is not paying attention to one's world at a place of complete absorption; something which can occur only if one has the capacity to focus fully on its details. As Aldous Huxley wrote in his iconic book *The Doors of Perception*, we of course have to learn how to effectively handle words and language; yet at the same time we must preserve and intensify our ability to look at the world directly, and not through what he calls "the half opaque medium of concepts," which he claims distort our experiences into all too familiar generic labels or explanatory abstractions.

Words and thoughts can become significant impediments to achieving the power of direct insight simply because they can serve as abstract barriers which serve to dull our perceptions and feelings by placing these into conceptual categories. So the question becomes how to not let this occur while at the same time still maintaining our ability to apprehend the details of the world clearly without becoming lost in a fog of irrelevancies.

Learning how to free ourselves from the energy draining activities of thought while clearly attending to our world through the clarity of direct perception, sensorial experience, and an emotive life in which our thoughts serve only to clarify, not impede. These would appear to be the preconditions for the development of a new intelligence born of direct insight, one that might become increasingly necessary for us to attain as the Internet and people's increasingly obsessive use of their digital devices continue to impede both the stream of our thoughts, our attention spans, and our working memories.

The question, of course, is how exactly to facilitate such an intelligence in people at a time in which the stream of their thoughts and their working memories are being ever more tightly conditioned by their use of digital technologies, and so the specific dynamics of thought and memory may be growing increasingly less clear. Perhaps, simply because such an intelligence might need to be built on a strong physiological, sensorial base, it might be wise to start there.

Chapter 3

Thought, Emotion, and the Physical Realm

In 1885, the Danish psychologist Carl Lange put forth the idea that unconscious emotion precedes conscious perception, but that the first stages of emotion are the body's responses to strong emotional stimuli, and that the conscious experience of emotion occurs only *after* the cerebral cortex has received signals about unconscious physiological events. In other words, according to Lange, someone experiences certain emotions only after their brain has received signals regarding relevant occurrences in the physical realm.

Then, in 1927, Harvard physiologist Walter B. Cannon, through his studies with both people and animals, expanded on Lange's theory by discovering that the intense emotion caused by either a perceived threat or a perceived reward triggers a primitive emergency response that mobilizes the body for action. Cannon described this response as "fight or flight." However, he likewise determined that such a physiological response cannot account for feelings that are specific to particular stimuli. Rather both responses (either "fight" or "flight") are simply the result of pure physiological reactions, such as dilated pupils or an increase in heart or respiratory rate.

More recently, however, there have been concerted attempts by researchers to more fully integrate emotion with physiology. In 2005, the late Dutch psychologist Nico Frijda expanded on the late American social psychologist Stanley Schacter's idea that a person's physiological response to events or situations is determined in part by the context in which they take place and the brain's reaction to it, by putting forth the theory that our conscious experience of emotion—what we feel—depends on where we focus our attention at any particular moment. Therefore, it seems possible that according to Frijda, attention, emotion, and physiology might be more integrally fused than what had been previously imagined.

Certainly, if our aim as human beings is to pursue a different type of intelligence, one born of a direct insight that exists beyond the intrinsic barriers of thought, memory, and language, then this fusion of physical responses, feelings, and attention would appear to be very much at the core of this search. In addition, as people's relentless use of their digital devices in accessing the Internet is something which is having a profound effect on their working memories and their stream of thought, then an immediate perception born of direct insight might easily become an essential means of dealing with the adverse effects which the Web may be having on our cognitive functions.

Of course, there are things which people can do right now to diminish the potential adverse effects of the Internet on their thoughts and memories. Rather than jump endlessly from one link to another while online, they can temporarily step away from their phone or PC in order to think carefully about the information or knowledge they've just digested in order that it can more easily become a part of their working memory.

When they can't remember something, rather than immediately downloading the information or knowledge on some large search engine, they can attempt to retrace their thoughts back toward another piece of information which might somehow be connected to that for which they are searching. That way the networks of thought in their brains that are relevant to the information or knowledge will not necessarily dry up or calcify.

Or they can take time each day to sit quietly and follow the stream of their thoughts wherever they might lead. By doing so, over time they will be able to see the difference between their natural progression and the jumpy, fragmented awareness by which the Web can easily condition those same thought processes.

Yet, at the same time, if we as humans can begin to increasingly access an immediate perception born of direct insight to better comprehend our world and ourselves as the Internet and our use of digital technologies continue to adversely affect our cognitive capacities, then we might potentially be able to continue acting intelligently regardless of the effects brought about by the present digital age.

Well-known Hungarian psychologist Mihaly Csikszentmihalyi has described in his writings a state of *flow* in which one becomes completely absorbed in whatever activity they are engaged because their particular skill level and the level of the task in which they are absorbed not only are perfectly matched, but likewise exist at a high level—a state of complete absorption which some have described as "being in the zone."

Csikszentmihalyi, in discussing creativity in relation to a state of *flow* in his book *Creativity: Flow and the Psychology of Discovery and Invention,* makes the point that creativity is the result of the interaction of three important components; the *individual* who has mastered a certain discipline; the specific cultural *domain* in which the individual is working; and the social *field* in which his creative endeavor exists.

In other words, creative acts require a larger social context in which they are appreciated and recognized by others. Creativity, rather than existing in isolation, is necessarily part of the specific social and intellectual environment in which someone is developing their creative endeavors. Even more importantly, there is nearly always a prior environment or set of circumstances upon which all creative endeavors are built.

Whether it's jazz musicians like Dexter Gordon building upon the impressionistic classical music of Debussy or Ravel; stream of consciousness writers such as Virginia Woolf building upon the exploration of the boundaries of the written word by Marcel Proust; Picasso expanding in his paintings the spatial ambiguity which Cezanne had originated; Einstein employing Hermann Minkowski's conception of four-dimensional space-time to develop his own great theory of General Relativity; or simply an architect using an approach to designing homes that one of his contemporaries has adopted, creativity is almost never something that comes out of nowhere. Almost always, it takes place within the context of past endeavors upon which it is built.

Therefore, the question would seem to be how we might facilitate a state of creative absorption, one that emanates from moments of direct insight and *flow* that lie beyond the intrinsic barriers of thought and memory, by determining how exactly it might be engendered in different areas of human endeavor by building upon the creative work of others.

The stream of consciousness writing that Jack Kerouac launched into the world, one which was highly sensorial and emotive in nature, took place during an artistic period in the Western world, particularly in New York City in the 1950s in which barriers which had previously blocked the expression of art through the solidity of forms were beginning to break down. For instance, by removing his brush from the canvas and instead painting vis-à-vis his method of *drip painting,* one in which he simply used his brush as a stick, Jackson Pollack had been able to transcend form with his paintings and instead allow a spontaneous expression of his self and his art to take place.

In similar fashion, Charly Parker developed through his brilliant saxophone playing a more formless approach to jazz that would come to be known as *bebop* when he was able to recognize that the twelve semitones of the chromatic scale could potentially lead melodically to any key. In doing so, by breaking through what had previously been the confines of a simpler jazz soloing, he was able to introduce melody lines with his playing that were much more complex simply because they had transcended the standard musical forms.

Kerouac, writing during this same period when the standard forms in any number of different artistic endeavors were beginning to dissipate and dissolve, developed his spontaneous approach to telling a story, as he put it, by simply sitting down at his typewriter and letting everything pour out of him without using the usual forms and structural techniques which had been previously employed by other writers to shape their stories in a preconceived manner.

In fact, when he wrote his famous book *On the Road,* one in which he depicted his adventures while endlessly traversing the country, he simply fed a long 120-foot roll of paper into his typewriter without having to stop to take out and replace separate sheets so that he could simply move forward in his mind with his book, without having to stop to shape his story into what he regarded as any sort of confining narrative form.

Therefore, Kerouac's unique approach to writing, one that had a profound effect on the future of American literature, took place within a larger social environment which encouraged a *flow state* to take place within him simply because other contemporaries of his were seriously experimenting at the time with the possibility of more formless expressions of their art taking place, *flow states* which were likewise being engendered in them by building upon the creative work of their contemporaries in other fields of artistic endeavor.

Likewise, just as cultural surroundings facilitate a flow state leading to creative exploration, so can actual physical surroundings. Csikszentmihalyi, in his book, makes mention of how Chinese sages chose to write their poetry on dainty island pavilions; Hindu Brahmins retreated to the forests to seek a reality which might be hidden behind appearances that were illusory; and Christian monks were so good at selecting spots which might engender their own forms of creativity that the hills or plains which drew their attention later became the sight of numerous convents and monasteries.

In short, both one's cultural and physical environments are often preconditions for germinating the sort of creativity that both stems from and likewise leads toward *flow*. Yet what about the inner physical realm of our minds and bodies? What effect might they have on such a development.

According to a paper by Manuela Macedonia, a neuroscientist at the University of Salzburg, *Embodied Learning: Why at School the Mind Needs the Body*, recent studies by neuroscientists and others have suggested that the mind is not an abstract and isolated entity, but that it is indeed integrated into the body's sensorimotor systems. In fact, various neuroscientific studies, such as those conducted by Friedemann Pulvermuller at Freie Universitat Berlin, have demonstrated that spatial information, music, faces, flavors, odors, and even mere thinking of these things evoke body-related activity in the brain.

Susan Greenfield, neuroscientist, bestselling author, and research fellow at Oxford University, writes in her recent book, *Mind Change: How Digital Technologies Are Leaving Their Mark on Our Brains*, about a study conducted by Alvaro Pascual-Leone, professor of neurology at Harvard Medical School. Pascual-Leone's research group found that during a five-day period in which a control group of subjects learned to play the piano using five-finger exercises, there was an astonishing change in their brain scans. What's more, and even more remarkable, they found that another group of subjects who were part of the same experiment and who were only required to imagine that they were playing the same exercises, showed almost identical changes in their scans.

What the results of these studies might seem to suggest is that not only does a sensory activity like playing music have a profound effect on the neuronal networks of our brains, but that there may be a deeper connection within our minds and brains between purely cognitive activities like imagination and memory and purely sensorial and emotive activities like listening to music or a simple walk in the woods than neuroscientists and others had previously imagined.

The question of course is how sensorial and emotive activities might become enhanced for the purpose of germinating an intelligence in which one can clearly perceive the various dynamics of their world beyond the boundaries of thought and memory. Furthermore, how exactly could such a process be facilitated?

Of course, what often occurs when we experience events in our lives which are of a predominately emotive or sensorial nature is that we tend to soon define them to ourselves in purely cognitive terms. That is, we use our thoughts to bring emotions or physical reactions fully to the surface of our conscious mind by either defining or rationalizing them. We likewise often use our thoughts to appraise our emotions, and by doing so put them into a certain perspective, one which we believe will allow us to better deal with them.

For example, we can make a potentially stressful situation, such as a test we're required to take, easier to deal with by telling ourselves that rather than being a judgment upon our self-worth, it is instead an opportunity for learning. Or we can view a disappointing outcome of a love affair as an opportunity to explore more fully who we really are rather than as a simple rejection. In other words, by using our thoughts, we often attempt to put a certain negative emotion into the sort of perspective which we hope will actually change its very nature for the better. The question is, however, what really occurs when we use our thoughts to redefine our feelings or our physical sensations?

Cognitive Behavioral Therapy, or CBT, seeks to understand the connection between our thoughts, our feelings, and our actions, in part through the supposition that as we understand how each of these three dynamics affects us, the more control we gain over our reactions. In other words, how we think about our emotions affects how we feel, and how we feel affects how we think or behave.

CBT tells us that it is more the thoughts about specific situations which have occurred in our lives, and not so much the actual situations themselves, which cause us to have certain feelings. Furthermore, many proponents of Cognitive Behavioral Therapy believe that the best place to start in terms of changing feelings or behaviors which are unacceptable or uncomfortable is with our thoughts. In other words, if we can change our thoughts, then we can better regulate our emotions or behaviors.

Yet at the same time there may be a certain fallacy in this belief that the best way to deal with emotions, or even physical reactions to situations, is through a reappraisal of them by our thoughts; this fallacy existing in opposition to the reality that when one feels a certain emotion, one "is" in fact that emotion. And by trying to change or redefine it, one is in fact only creating conflict within oneself. Whereas, if one is able to fully inhabit a particular emotion at the time it occurs, one is by fully embodying it allowing oneself to remain whole and free of conflict.

That is to say, at the moment in which one feels jealous of someone or something, there is only jealousy, and that by trying to deal with the negative feeling of jealousy by suppressing it, or by reappraising it or rationalizing it with one's thoughts or memories, one is only moving ever further from the reality of it, and in the process producing internal conflict. Whereas, on the contrary, if one is able to sit with the feeling of jealousy, without trying to change it, define it, or rationalize it with one's thoughts in any way, then the possibility exists that the negative emotion may begin to dissipate and eventually disappear; potentially even turning into a larger reality born of a quiet mind.

Krishnamurti spoke often of how the observer *is* the observed, and the metaphysical philosopher Alan Watts often mentioned in his writings how the thinker is the thought. What both of them are alluding to is how the separation between an experiencer and what they experience creates unnecessary division and fragmentation in people in a way that causes them to be in conflict with themselves.

Krishnamurti said that when there is complete cessation of division between the observer and the observed, then "what is" is no longer simply "what is" but is transformed into something much larger. And Alan Watts in his book *The Wisdom of Insecurity* mentioned how people impede the flow of events in their lives by endlessly trying to control them within a framework of fixed ideas, rather than recognizing that these events might in fact be representative of a larger reality that exists within the flux of events from our daily lives, provided that one is willing to surrender to it.

Therefore, a holistic approach to intelligence which seeks to fuse emotions and sensorial reactions with the events which spawned them might begin to not only eliminate this same division and conflict in people—a fragmentation which causes them to view the events in their lives less clearly—but likewise might lead toward the potential apprehension of a larger consciousness born of direct insight, one which may exist on the other side of thought and memory.

Yet before such a holistic intelligence which might fully integrate our perceptions of our world with both our emotions and our sensorial reactions to it can be fully understood, it would appear to be necessary to examine exactly how the spatial map in our brain, that which is the result of long-term memories and which allows us to formulate a clear internal picture of our world, operates in terms of not only cognitive occurrences, but likewise how it might operate in terms of emotive and sensorial ones.

At the same time, however, if both our short and long-term memories are being adversely affected by the sort of overload that has now become a significant part of how we apprehend information and knowledge in the digital age, then it seems necessary to ask how that might affect the potentially clear picture of our world that is part of our interior life. Furthermore, how might that potentially negative development likewise affect an endeavor to fuse feelings and sensorial occurrences with one's perceptions of the world in the search for a larger intelligence?

Chapter 4

Thought, Memory, and Our Interior World

The spatial map in the hippocampus region of our brain is essentially an internal picture we create of our world, one that aids us in selectively attending to parts of our immediate environment. It is also what allows us to not only create long-term memories, but to have access to them later. Without such a clear internalization, it would become more difficult to selectively attend to important elements of our world while at the same time blocking out irrelevant ones. Ultimately our capacity to learn from our experience is adversely affected when we can no longer attend to what knowledge and information is important for us to absorb.

Therefore, both the spatial map and our long-term memories are key components of what permits us to focus clearly on the details of our world. Otherwise, if we were less able to sort out what is significant from what is irrelevant, we would never be able to experience the dynamics of our world in any sort of clear-sighted manner. Consequently, we would become less able to think clearly about our experiences, and so would become less able to discern what our feelings or sensorial occurrences might be telling us. Eventually, we might well wander around in a fog of unclear, meaningless experience.

One question of course is if the spatial map in our brain only provides us with a clear, internalized picture of our world that is based solely on thought and memory, or if it might be able to provide us with the same internal mapping of our world based likewise on emotions and sensorial occurrences without requiring that we define those feelings and sensorial events with our thinking minds? And as a corollary, the question that might need to be asked is if there is a potential understanding of our world through a holistic intelligence that fuses attention with emotions and physical sensations without relying on the process of thought to define those things for us.

A large part of the answer to these questions certainly has to do with the capacity of both the spatial map and our long-term memory to selectively filter out irrelevant information and knowledge by attending only to that which is deemed to be either significant or important. Therefore, what exact role might selective attention play in allowing us to correctly absorb the details of our world through a more holistic intelligence in which we are able to become fully absorbed in our feelings and senses?

Long-term memory certainly has a role to play in selective attention, serving as a bridge between our perceptions of the details of our world and our potential actions. For example, campers in a wilderness area in which there have been reports of the sighting of a mountain lion and her cubs must use their capacity for selective attention to keep themselves safe by paying attention to only what is significant in their immediate environment while at the same time ignoring irrelevant details.

That is, they should most definitely pay attention to any tracks they have discovered walking certain trails while at the same time ignoring the activity of other animals for whom the mountain lion would not have any interest as a food source, such as the calls of certain birds.

On the other hand, how might those same campers deal with this situation without having to define for themselves what is significant and what is not vis-à-vis their cognitive processes of thought and memory; instead using only their emotive and sensorial capabilities? Would they be able to comprehend exactly why the sounds of certain animals might be important to listen to while the sounds of others are irrelevant without having to necessarily use their working memory or their rational mind to sort out the significant differences; the answer to this question potentially existing within moments in which the emotive and sensorial lives of the campers are fused into moments of creative absorption and direct insight.

This type of fully absorbed emotive or sensorial experience obviously exists at a deeper level than that which exists solely in the realm of thought and memory simply because it is not diluting experience by holding it at arm's length in order to examine it. Rather, it is a type of intelligence which arrives purely and directly in the moment in a manner which fully engages both feelings and reactions to physical sensations.

This is the sort of intelligence which animals use by allowing their feelings and sensorial lives to direct their movements through the world. Because most members of the animal kingdom, with the possible exception of primates far up the evolutionary scale such as gorillas or chimpanzees, are most likely not capable of self-reflective thought, this type of physical intelligence becomes their guide.

Yet how might a holistic intelligence in which one becomes fully absorbed in emotions or physical sensations work in our human world? How might a direct insight which takes place on the other side of thought and memory potentially assist people in engendering a clear perception of events and other people, a perception which leads toward a more intelligent apprehension of the world than that which purely cognitive processes such as thought and memory might be able to provide?

There is a great scene in the film *Adaptation*, based on Susan Orlean's popular book *The Orchid Thief*, in which the character of John Laroche, an orchid expert played by Chris Cooper, introduces Orlean, played by Meryl Streep, to a whole other level of intelligence than one might suspect is taking place while one is watching insects pollinating flowers. What Laroche explains so passionately to Orlean is how every flower has a specific relationship with the insect that is pollinating it, in effect the flower being the insect's soul mate, its double.

Therefore, the insect wants nothing more than to make love to the flower by pollinating it. At the same time, although neither the insect nor the flower can ever understand the significance of their little dance with each other, the world comes alive because of it. Then going on to explain the larger significance of what is occurring, Laroche tells Orlean that because both the insect and the flower are doing exactly what they are designed to do, something magnificent happens. That is, they show us how to live; how the only barometer one has is their heart, and that once you spot your flower, so to speak, you can't let anything get in your way.

What John Laroche is doing in his remarkable soliloquy is becoming fully absorbed in a moment of direct insight originating in a world beyond words or explanations; one which moves steadily from a description of how insects choose the flower they will pollinate to how the entire world lives whenever an animal, human, or even plant follows their moment of direct desire.

In similar fashion, a middle-aged woman visits her aging father, who is now living alone after his wife, the woman's mother, has recently died. When the woman visits him, she can see how unhappy he is due to his loneliness, and likewise due to a lack of purpose in his life. Therefore, she begins to feel a great amount of pity for him, and even for herself as his daughter. However, on one of her visits to her father, she is able to experience beyond the bounds of thought or memory, an enormous feeling of sorrow not just for her father, but for all those people in the world who are likewise lonely and unfulfilled. And so she leaves her father on that particular day with that same feeling of deep sorrow within her.

Several nights later, as the woman is sitting alone in her kitchen late at night while experiencing the same feeling of deep sorrow for her father and others, that sorrow begins to expand into a feeling of real compassion for all those in the world who are struggling with whatever life has dealt them. Later, that same night, with that feeling of compassion for others still filling her completely, she walks into the backyard where she lives in the country and gazes up at the stars. While doing so, she experiences in that moment her feeling of compassion for others turn to an awareness of how incredibly special life is, even something that might be called sacred. Later, as she goes back inside and prepares for bed, that feeling of the sacredness of life remains with her.

In a manner similar to John Laroche's soliloquy on the relationship between direct desire and the totality of life in the world, this woman's capacity to become fully absorbed in her original moment of pity for her father, and then by following that feeling through a selective attention existing on the other side of thoughts and words toward sorrow, compassion, and then the sacredness of life, her consciousness was able to move toward a larger intelligence concerning life in the world.

Selective attention is obviously a key in moving in this same fashion through the sensory and emotive worlds within oneself toward a larger intelligence which isn't necessarily apprehended through words and thoughts, but rather through heightened sensory and emotive experience. In addition, it should be rather obvious that John Laroche and the woman visiting her aging father, in addition to using their power of selective attention, were most likely existing in a state similar to that of *flow*.

According to Arne Dietrich, professor of psychology at the American University, Beirut, Lebanon, *flow* has been associated with decreased activity in the prefrontal cortex of the brain, an area responsible for higher cognitive functions such as self-reflection, consciousness, memory, and temporal integration. Quite simply, it's an area that is responsible for our conscious and explicit states of mind, those which allow us to make conscious choices in thinking clearly about our world by focusing on certain aspects of it.

However, in a state of *flow*, this area of the brain is believed to temporarily down-regulate in a process called *transient hypofrontality*; triggering feelings of distortion of time, loss of self-consciousness, and loss of an inner critic; this inhibition of the prefrontal lobe then allowing the implicit mind, that which does not require conscious attention in order to recall something (e.g. habitual thoughts and behaviors) to assist certain brain areas in more freely communicating with each other.

Implicit memory has been identified as a key functional region of the brain in terms of *flow* because it reduces verbal-analytical involvement in motor control by encouraging limited dependence on explicit memory, that which requires a focused conscious attention. Whereas the automatic nature of implicit memory, such as what takes place in habitual behaviors like signing one's name or riding a bike, is often fast, effortless, and free from distraction.

Furthermore, if it was in fact determined that this automatic, implicit process which occurs in a state of flow allows different areas of the brain to more easily interact with one another because there is less interference between them, then this would appear to give credence to how a state of *flow* might be a genuine key in engendering a more holistic, integrated intelligence in which emotions, physical sensations, states of attention, and states of perception become interconnected in producing moments of direct insight existing on the other side of thought and memory.

Until fairly recently, the prevailing view of brain connectivity focused only on whether or not two different regions of the brain were connected, not the strength or distance of the connections. Yet, according to researchers such as Henry Kennedy, researcher at the Stem-cell and Brain Research Institute in France, the brain is actually a densely connected network in which about 70 percent of specific areas are connected to every other area. This new understanding of different brain regions, according to Kennedy, hints at how the brain is wired not just by regions, but down to the level of single neurons.

In addition, according to Nicholas Turk-Browne, professor of cognitive science at Yale University, different brain functions are distributed across different brain areas, and are not confined to a single region; consequently, any complex behavior requires interaction between the different areas.

Therefore, if regions of the brain are more thoroughly connected to one another than what was previously thought by neuroscientists and others to be the case, then how might a state of *flow* engender increased connections between specific areas of the brain, and how might certain human behaviors enhance such a flow state through brain connectivity? Both of these questions, it would seem, would appear to be critical in connecting not just a flow state, but mind and brain connectivity itself to the search for a more expansive intelligence; questions which will be further examined as this work proceeds.

Perhaps one answer might lay in how one organizes the spatial-temporal structure of the world in which one lives in order, as Mihaly Csikszentmihalyi says, to cultivate a state of *flow* in their everyday life. In his book *Creativity*, Csikszentmihalyi uses as an example of this structuring of one's physical environment like the home of a Hindu Brahman or a traditional Japanese family, which are likely to be bare of almost all furniture and decoration; the idea being that these remain neutral environments that do not disturb the flow of consciousness with potential distractions.

In a 2009 paper on *flow*, Jeanne Nakamura, professor of Behavioral and Organizational Sciences at Claremont Graduate University, and Mihaly Csikszentmihalyi made mention of how important it was to understand that one can't experience *flow* if distractions disrupt the experience. Therefore, in order to experience a state of flow, one might need to stay away as much as possible from the attention robbers that have become common in our contemporary lives, such as smartphones and other digital devices.

Once again, long-term memory is important for maintaining a focused attention simply because it allows one to distinguish between information that is relevant to one's area of immediate concern, and that which is irrelevant. Furthermore, when one's short-term memory is overwhelmed with too much information, as is happening in today's digital age as people are becoming increasingly overwhelmed by the amount of information coming at them on the Web, then short-term memory, which has a limited storage capacity, is less able to pass it on to one's long-term memory.

As one can imagine, one's capacity for maintaining a focused attention, one that is able to sort out the relevant from the irrelevant, is highly dependent on one's short-term memory not succumbing to information overload. In addition, because our long-term memory is responsible for our ability to conceptualize, to turn information into concepts and ideas, when our working memory becomes overtaxed, we lose a significant amount of our ability to think intelligently about our world.

Therefore, in an age of information overload, what role might the type of holistic intelligence discussed in this work—one that integrates emotions, sensorial reactions, and states of attention into a unified state of creative absorption—play in allowing us to maintain our optimal capacity to focus and to see our world clearly? In other words, is it possible that because this state of creative absorption engenders a direct insight in which one grows ever more able to clearly apprehend certain truths concerning one's world on the other side of thought and memory, information overload might over time become increasingly less of a negative factor in our mental lives?

The spatial map which allows us to not only internalize and structure the elements of our world, our experiences, and even our own thought processes so that we can learn from them is a vital part of our mental life, one which allows us to see things clearly and to behave intelligently. Yet to date it has been based mainly on our thought processes. However, if our intelligence were to become one which was increasingly based on direct insight, rather than one that is largely a matter of rational thought and working memory, as it now is, how might our internalization of our world function in a new age whose primary characteristics are creative absorption and immediate perception? This is where we will head next.

Chapter 5

Insight, Attention, and Creative Absorption

Eric Kandel in *The Age of Insight* focuses on the work of John Kounios, professor of psychology at Drexel University and Mark Jung-Beeman, professor of psychology at Northwestern University, who while working together discovered that creative insight is in fact the culmination of a series of transient brain states operating at different locations in the brain and over different lengths of time, even though the moment of insight may have occurred suddenly and appears to be disconnected from whatever thoughts might have preceded it.

Jung-Beeman also believes that a certain relaxation phase is necessary for the moment of direct insight, the *aha* phenomenon, to exist; arguing that once the brain significantly attends to solving a particular problem, it then needs to relax so that it might be able to put itself in touch with other possible solutions. Jung-Beeman also says that when a person is actively trying to solve a problem through creative insight, he or she needs to concentrate but also let the mind wander, that is move away from a state of intense concentration, either when the person is stalled at a place of impasse or else first formulating the problem in their mind.

In terms of focusing on a work of art, according to Jung-Beeman, although one by necessity needs to focus on the work to the exclusion of everything else, at the same time if one focuses on the details of a painting or other artwork too intently, rather than attempting to take in the overall picture by letting one's mind wander over it, then that can disrupt one's insight into its essence.

31

If creative insight is dependent on both a resting state in the brain during which someone perceives a problem they are attempting to solve or a work of art through a more expansive apprehension, and if insight often occurs only after certain mental activities have been given different periods of time to develop, then what might this portend for the development of a holistic intelligence in which different emotional or sensorial activities are effectively integrated with perceptions of one's world to produce moments of true insight?

Quite possibly, it could mean that moments of insight tend to occur only when certain personal experiences—be they emotive, sensorial, or perceptual—have been given a significant period of time to become absorbed at different rates by the brain before they are fused together as one into an *aha* moment of creative absorption. Furthermore, such a moment of immediate understanding might occur in a surprising, unasked for fashion when the circumstances of one's life come together to meld the three types of experience.

For example, a certain artist may have had a strong emotive experience upon being rejected by another person or group of people relative to something in which he believed deeply, for instance a work of art upon which he has spent considerable time. The wound from the rejection having to do with the amount of time the artist has spent attempting to create the work of art might be particularly deep because the rejection is known by an entire group of other artists whom the artist knows well, a dynamic which the artist who has suffered the rejection has thought about at length, and by which he is embarrassed.

One afternoon, several weeks after experiencing the rejection, the artist is walking near a large concert hall in the city where he lives and hears some beautiful organ music coming from inside. At the same time, the shadows of two winged statues appear on the pavement in front of him. Then, just as the exquisite organ music reaches its apex and comes to an end, the sudden appearance of bright sunlight overhead dissipates the shadows of the winged statues as they disappear into a moment of soothing warmth and brightness.

The artist, through a moment of creative insight which has suddenly arrived, sees clearly in the moment exactly how his artistic work can be opened into something much larger and more expansive by leaving behind what he had previously visualized it to be. In other words, the combination of the emotive quality of the beautiful organ music, the sensorial experience of the sudden appearance of the bright sunlight, and the perceptual experience of the dissipation of the shadows of the winged statues have all come together in an instant to produce his moment of creative absorption and direct insight.

Most likely, if the artist had simply tried to think his way into a different approach to his work of art, one that might produce something that was more fully realized, he might well have run into the same cognitive barrier which he had previously come up against in creating his work simply because he would only be summoning something from the past to produce something new in the future, rather than being able in his moment of direct insight to leave the past entirely behind in order to create a new vision for his art that was taking place entirely in the present.

At the same time, his sudden moment of insight might well have, unbeknownst to him, been evolving within him over a period of time, and consequently needed only the organ music, the shadows of the winged statues, and the appearance of the bright sunlight to appear in a particular moment in order to fully release his new vision.

In addition, his unique vision may very well have been a product of the work of other artists even though this may have been something that he didn't fully realize at the time simply because those other works of art resided within him at an entirely unconscious level. Given the right circumstances, those visions or thoughts which had been a part of his unconscious memory were brought to the forefront of his conscious attention, and so he was able in his moment of insight to visualize something entirely new.

For example, perhaps he was a sculptor who wasn't able to produce the work he had envisioned because he was having difficulties with the space in which his particular piece might exist relative to its different parts. Having previously studied the work of Georges Braque, the twentieth-century French painter and sculptor whose work significantly influenced Picasso, particularly his linking of the properties of visual and tactile space in his work, the artist may have been able to recall the work of Braque just as he was apprehending the shadows of the winged statues on the ground in front of him, and consequently the bright sunlight caused them to dissipate and pass in his mind into something larger.

Therefore, in addition to the emotive apprehension of the beautiful organ music, and the intense sensorial experience of the bright sunlight and shadows, there may have been an unconscious memory of Braque's work still residing within him, even though he might not have been consciously aware of it for an extended period of time. This then may have contributed to his moment of creative absorption, and to a solution to his dilemma through an insight that was brought fully to the fore vis-à-vis his sudden apprehension of what had just occurred within him sensorially and emotively to produce a solution to his problem.

A fully embodied emotive experience fused with an intense sensorial visualization, brought to the fore through the catalyst of an unconscious memory, and then fully realized through a sudden awareness of what had just taken place within him—these were the different components that were effectively fused together within the artist to produce his moment of insight.

On the other hand, if he had tried to use his rational thought processes to think his way into a different way to visualize his sculpture, depended entirely on his conscious memories of what other artists had produced, or even gone online to surf the Web looking for examples of the work of other sculptors that he could study which might have been relevant, he might very well have reached some sort of creative impasse simply by being trapped in the past relative to his own experience and likewise the experience of others.

What may also be highly relevant to the sculptor's experience of creative absorption is that most likely the different elements—emotive, sensorial, perceptual—may have been evolving within him over different periods of time, but then came together in an instant to produce his *aha* moment of direct insight. Therefore, the question would appear to be what might be learned from this example in examining how a similar process might be employed to facilitate moments of creative absorption and direct insight in a digital age in which the powers of rational thought and working memory are likely going to continue to dissipate?

In the case of many great artists, there is often a significant period of time between when their unique vision begins to take shape within them and then when they are able to eventually bring it to fruition through a moment of creative insight. For example, Pablo Picasso's work on what would become his breakthrough painting *Les Demoiselles d'Avignon* had reached a standstill in 1907 with the artist being confused concerning how he might present the same subjects from multiple perspectives. However, after visiting the *Musee Ethnologie* at Trocadero, Spain following a recommendation that he do so by the painter Derain and being significantly affected at an emotive level by some African masks which were on display there, he returned to his studio.

Having recently studied the work of the French physicist Henri Poincare concerning the possibility of a four-dimensional space, and making an immediate connection between those ideas and the African masks he had observed relative to how a single subject might be observed from multiple perspectives, and with Cezanne's still life paintings drawn from four different perspective points still a part of his working memory, Picasso was able by geometrizing space through a multiplicity of different viewpoints shown simultaneously to produce his masterpiece from his moment of insight.

In doing so, he was able to combine the emotive effect on him brought about by the sensorial quality which the African masks presented with his intuitive understanding of four-dimensional space as a result of his studies of Poincare, and by using what he had learned from the work of Cezanne, to bring his new vision of geometry and space to fruition in producing his iconic painting showing various female figures from different perspectives and points of view. That is, his moment of creative absorption was able to take place within him specifically because the emotive and sensorial aspects of his creative intelligence were effectively integrated with his cognitive understanding of how space might operate in another dimension.

Of course, few people possess the genius of a Picasso. Yet at the same time through an increased attentiveness to the details of the world and our own minds, many of us can solve problems that have been plaguing us in both our personal and professional lives, bring new, radically different ideas into the world, or be more creative in attending to the dynamics of our close personal relationships.

A psychological state of complete attention, that in which the observer and the observed are one and the same, would appear to present the best possibility for effectively fusing the emotive and the sensorial into a larger, holistic intelligence simply because it is a state in which there is little or no separation between the personal and the nonpersonal; what Aldous Huxley described during his experience with the consciousness expanding drug mescaline as "a *Not-self*" simultaneously perceiving and being the *Not-self* of the things around me."

When one is able to become fully absorbed in the dynamics of people, situations, or objects which exist in one's world, the habitual tendency to hold those people, situations, or objects at arm's length, so to speak, in order to examine them from a cognitive standpoint, even if only momentarily, begins to disappear, and instead one is more able to be in touch with the emotive and sensorial qualities which those things represent.

In his iconic book *The Doors of Perception*, Aldous Huxley describes some window drapes not just as something that provide an element of privacy inside one's home, but as a silken wilderness of a countless number of tiny pleats and wrinkles; and the folds in his trousers as being not just part of a necessary article of clothing, but a labyrinth of endlessly significant complexity.

Naturally, in order to remain functional in the world which one inhabits, one must be able to use the power of representational thought. Otherwise, one might begin to psychologically drown in a world which one has lost the ability to effectively hold at bay and conceptualize with his thinking mind. Whether it's the dynamics inherent in one's personal life, the larger social dynamics taking place around one, or simply various elements of the natural world with which one is engaged, one often necessarily needs to maintain the capacity to understand these cognitively at a level that makes them as clear and accessible as they might potentially be.

Yet at a level of deeper relationship, one might potentially see more clearly the elements of one's world and come into closer contact with them if one is observing them at a place of complete attention in which the observer and the observed become one. That is, in which the psychological distance between that with which one is coming into contact and one's self begins to shrink exponentially, possibly even evaporate completely.

Frances Crick, the discoverer of the structure of DNA along with James Watson, spent much of the latter part of his life studying the dynamics of visual perception; coming to believe that while we may form a picture of the visual world in our brain, we also have a symbolic representation of that same world. Crick's investigations of the subject follow from the musings of Richard Gregory, a British psychologist of the twentieth and twenty-first centuries who investigated the role of knowledge pertaining to visual perception and illusions.

Gregory investigated the question of when we see something like a tree, does a tree-like picture necessarily already exist in the brain, that which allows us to see *tree*? The conclusion he came to is that this is just not the case. Rather the brain only has hypotheses about objects in the outside world that reflect the conscious experience of seeing them. In the case of optical illusions, certain hypotheses which one has formed in his or her brain cause a specific perception to be altered significantly from what it might otherwise be.

If it is indeed the case that it is not necessary for a predetermined image of something to exist in the mind in order for it to register as a viable object of perception, but rather the object of perception is the result of certain hypotheses the brain has formed from memory concerning the particular image which brings the object to fruition, then this would appear to give credence to the idea that our feelings and perceptions may to a certain extent be the result of ideas and memories we have developed over time, and which affect the reality of what we feel and see.

This of course begs the question of what we might otherwise see and feel if our perceptions and feelings were pure and devoid of interference from our mental life? Of course, a corollary to this would be how often do our predetermined thoughts, ideas, and hypotheses about the world actually determine what we see and feel? If the answer to this question is that our cognitive lives do in fact often determine in advance much of what we see and feel, then is there in fact some way to avoid that so that our perceptions and feelings might remain free from the interfering conjectures and hypotheses of our thoughts?

As is true with those children who have developed the ability to conceptualize their world, our perceptual and sensorial experiences as adults tend to occur prior to our ability to conceptualize them. That is, we tend to see and feel things purely and directly, even if only momentarily, before we attempt to make sense of what we have just experienced through our thoughts and long-term memories.

However, the impressionistic lives of most children (their capacity to see and feel things) often tend to exist at a more intense level of clarity and depth than our own, even though they might not be able to express this verbally, simply because their adeptness at conceptualizing their world hasn't yet come to full fruition. Therefore, because thoughts and memories don't tend to impede their experiences and impressions of the world at the same level that they tend to do with adults, children often tend to have a more pure, more direct experience of their world.

Naturally, the question that would appear to follow from this is whether adults might be able to experience their world as they once did as children while at the same time maintaining their ability to concep-tualize it fully. Or to pursue the matter further, is there an intelligence in which we have full access to our thoughts and memories, yet at the same time retain the capacity to experience our world at the same level of impressionistic depth that we once enjoyed as children?

Once again, Alan Watts wrote of the possibility of a deeper reality that exists on the other side of the events of our daily lives, a *stream of life* he called it that he claims we continually impede by conceptualizing the occurrences in our lives into fixed ideas that keep us separated from that more expansive reality of which those occurrences are a part. The question of course is how one might allow oneself to surrender to that organic stream while yet maintaining one's capacity to conceptualize and think intelligently about the particulars of one's world whenever that particular ability is needed?

Recently, a team of researchers whose findings were published in 2019 by the American Psychological Association proposed the idea of what they called *forward flow*, which they termed as being the average semantic distance between any given thought and all previous thoughts. This they did by using what they called latent semantic analysis to attempt to capture how thoughts evolve over time (i.e., how thoughts in the present moment differ from thoughts which have occurred in the past). Likewise, they endeavored to examine whether the concept of forward flow can be used to predict creative thinking in both the lab and the real world.

What seems interesting about this particular endeavor is that the researchers were in fact attempting to examine a flow state similar to that which Mihaly Csikszentmihalyi and Alan Watts have alluded from the outside, so to speak, by subjecting it to objective scientific analysis, and to likewise objectively linking the occurrence of *flow* to the creative process itself; particularly in terms of the idea that *forward flow*, in addition to being understood as the semantic distance between present and past thoughts can likewise be understood as the capacity for a stream of consciousness to flow forward, leaving previous thoughts entirely behind.

In addition, researchers have found that forward motion in our thoughts is highly predictive of creativity. That is, people with a higher degree of forward flow tend to give more creative answers to standard creativity tasks, as well as engaging in more creative careers (e.g., artists, writers, entrepreneurs, those creating something new in their particular area of professional expertise) than those people who are part of the general population.

What exactly is the relationship between creativity and the stream of thought? How might the stream of our thoughts become part of a larger intelligence which is effectively integrated with our emotive and sensorial lives? These are obviously questions which would seemingly need to be addressed if neuroscientists, psychologists, educators, and others are to investigate the possibility of a holistic intelligence which allows us to perceive the details of our world through direct insight rather than rely so much on our rational mind and working memories in a digital age in which these are being significantly diminished. Therefore, this is where we will turn next in attempting to examine what the exact relationship might be between a creative mind and the stream of our thoughts.

Chapter 6

Creativity and the
Stream of Thought

For creative thinking to take place it often needs to exist in a psychological space in which the mind is able to make significant connections between different knowledge and information without any sort of interruption or distraction preventing those connections from being realized. Otherwise, the degree of creative absorption necessary for making those connections will be inherently missing.

In addition, it is particularly important that in apprehending information creatively, one is able to see similar dynamics or truths existing in different areas of knowledge. That is to say, the creative person is often able to extend knowledge that they may have acquired in one subject area to other areas of inquiry, even if those two areas of inquiry might on the surface appear to be significantly different.

In terms of the stream of thought and forward flow, the creative person needs to be able to move forward with his thinking, rather than remain fixated on past thoughts, yet at the same time maintain the ability to make significant connections whenever necessary between those past thoughts and where the forward flow of his thinking mind might be taking him in the present.

Yet how does one avoid the trap of being caught in the web of those previous thoughts to the point where they prevent one from seeing something entirely new even though those new original thoughts proceed inevitably from where his creative mind has taken him in the past? In other words, how does one build on what one has discovered in the past while moving into uncharted waters? And how does one learn to effortlessly follow the stream of their thoughts without impeding it with thoughts, ideas, and conjectures from the past while still building on those?

In addition, relative to the subject of this book, how might one fuse one's sensorial and emotive experiences with the stream of one's thoughts in a manner which further clarifies those thoughts to the point where one can occasionally leave them behind, and instead apprehend the details and dynamics of one's world through the power of direct insight?

The late Canadian psychologist Donald O. Hebb, who was instrumental in investigating how the function of neuron assemblies in the brain contributes to psychological processes such as thought and learning and who believed that everything in the brain is interrelated and works together, likewise determined that for there to be a moment of true creative insight, the task involved needs to possess just the right degree of difficulty for the person having the insight.

Hebb's ideas on direct insight, in which one is entirely absorbed in a certain activity, are obviously similar to what Mihaly Csikszentmihalyi has to say about a flow state, which he postulated can only occur when the challenge of the task and the skill level of the person are equally matched at a certain level of complexity.

The ideas of Hebb and Csikszentmihalyi on creative absorption might mean that if one is to in fact experience a moment of direct insight and absorption, that moment might be significantly engendered if one's perceptions, sensorial experiences, and emotions have reached a point of fruition where the person is able to creatively absorb the complexity of his unique experience simply because these particular dynamics have all reached their maximum potential. Therefore, in being effectively integrated with one another, they're able to match the complexity of an experience in producing a moment of true insight.

In his book *Creating Minds,* Howard Gardner writes of how although much creative work actually involves the solution of problems which are already recognized as being significant within the particular field or domain in which one works, higher level creative work is characterized by what he calls the fashioning of a new area of concern, or by the discovery of a previously unknown or neglected set of issues that require fresh exploration.

Although Gardner is speaking primarily of artists, scientists, or other individuals adding some new vision to, or some new way of approaching the particular domain in which they work, it would appear that the same could be said for original moments of creative insight evolving in individuals even though they may be momentary experiences. That is, looking at some aspect of one's world with entirely fresh eyes which suggest some new way of apprehending things at a place beyond both thought and memory.

Because thought and memory, by themselves, are products of the past, our thinking minds are always swinging back and forth between past and future; this movement necessarily excluding anything entirely new occurring within us simply because how we envision the future is nearly always a product of the past; meaning that if one is to perceive something with entirely fresh eyes, that perception must occur beyond that place in our minds where the future is somehow a projection of our past experiences.

Yet if thought is fundamentally a product of our past experiences, rather than an apprehension of something entirely new, what dynamics would tend to make moments of direct insight something entirely new rather than mere projections of the past? Furthermore, what might be significant to consider here is what role a holistic intelligence in which one's emotive and sensorial lives are effectively integrated with one's cognitive life might play in allowing people to live more fully in the present moment.

Most researchers now believe that the brain can continue to form new neural pathways throughout a person's life in response to environmental stimuli, a concept known as neuroplasticity. As Susan Greenfield says, it is the continuous growth and connections between different brain cells which we are born with which turn us into the unique beings we become. In addition, not only is the brain continually shifting in response to the inputs of one's environment, but it is likewise shifting in response to its own responses; something which makes the brain an organ of almost unlimited potential for change.

According to a paper published in 2017 by The Royal Society, an independent scientific academy in the UK dedicated to promoting excellence in science for the benefit of humanity, one of the more interesting developments in intelligence research lately has been the finding that performance on sets of seemingly disparate tasks have been positively correlated with one another. For example, individuals who perform above average on visual perception also tend to perform above average on something like word definition.

Therefore, what might those particular findings suggest in terms of brain plasticity and the capacity over time for seemingly different areas related to cognition, emotions, or sensorial experiences to effectively integrate with one another?

In an article published in 2020 by Branton Shearer, an independent researcher and clinical neuropsychologist, in the *Journal of the American Psychological Association* concerning functional connectivity in the brain related to implications for multiple intelligences theory, Shearer's investigation reviewed forty-eight functionally connected cognitive neuroscience studies involving the resting brain.

Seven to fifteen neural networks in the brain were found to be well aligned with seven of eight multiple intelligences, as well as with intelligence in general; the same neural networks that had been previously identified by past research as the neural bases for multiple intelligence. These results, according to the study, then demonstrated that each person possesses unique latent neural potentials aligned with the various forms of multiple intelligence.

Once again, Howard Gardner's theory of multiple intelligences postulated that people possess not just cognitive intelligence, but also a number of different types of intelligence, such as logical/mathematical, linguistic, musical, spatial, bodily/kinesthetic, naturalist, interpersonal, and intrapersonal. Gardner also writes in his book that we all have various forms of these different intelligences, but that they may differ in us individually based on our genetic makeup and our life experience.

What might be interesting to consider in terms of how Gardner's theory of multiple intelligences might relate to various forms of neural connectivity in a human brain that researchers are increasingly coming to understand possesses a high degree of plasticity, is how different brain networks might be effectively integrated with each other for the purpose of engendering not only *aha* moments of direct insight and creative absorption, but likewise a larger, more holistic intelligence.

A new framework for understanding changes in the brain's activity and connections was developed in 2020 by researchers at Georgia State University; the study building on previous works showing that the shape and connectivity of brain networks—discrete areas of the brain that work together to perform complex cognitive tasks—can change in fundamental and recurring ways over time.

Referencing the concept of *spatiotemporal dynamics*, which refers both to changes in the shape, size, or location of brain networks, and likewise to changes in the connections between various networks, the researchers put forth the idea that spatiotemporal dynamics is how the brain needs to be studied because it takes in simultaneously changes in regard to not only the shape, size, and location of networks, but also in terms of their connectivity with one another.

Looking at the human brain in this more holistic manner—in which the dynamics of different areas and their relationship to one another are considered simultaneously—might then open new opportunities for the consideration of a more integrated intelligence in which various areas of human endeavor related to perception, emotion, sensorial, and cognitive experience are seen as being fused together in moments of creative insight. In addition, this more holistic view might then lead toward new approaches in education which facilitate such insight, and likewise greater creativity.

In addition, some of the multiple intelligences elucidated by Howard Gardner may be able to be more effectively combined with one another through various means which not only provide a blueprint of sorts for how they might be successfully fused into a larger intelligence, but likewise might serve as guidelines for how to actually integrate them with one another, particularly in terms of different areas that have traditionally been seen as essentially disparate.

For example, naturalist intelligence, which involves understanding living things and reading nature, might be somehow fused with spatial intelligence, which involves visualizing the world in 3-D, to provide more creative approaches to saving our environment in the age of global warning. Logical-mathematical intelligence, which involves quantifying things, making hypotheses, and proving them might be combined with linguistic intelligence in order to engender more creative ways to better express bottom-line truths vis-à-vis our ever-changing digital world.

Or intrapersonal intelligence, which has to do with understanding oneself, what one feels and what one's desires are, might be effectively integrated with bodily-kinesthetic intelligence having to do with coordinating one's mind and body to produce creative approaches to activities like meditation or yoga that might allow one to understand oneself well enough to occasionally peek over the edge of the personal self in search of a larger, more expansive consciousness.

Needless to say, there is still much to be learned by neuroscientists, psychologists, and others concerning the issue of connectivity in general, brain connectivity and otherwise, and how different areas of our psyches, emotions, and sensorial lives might be effectively integrated with one another to produce new approaches to creatively apprehending one's world. As much as anything, the limitations of thought, the thinking mind, and memory need to be examined more carefully so that one's cognitive life doesn't impede one's emotive or sensorial life from coming to full fruition.

As anyone who is even tangentially familiar with quantum physics already knows, Werner Heisenberg's uncertainty principle states that one can't know the momentum and the position of a subatomic particle simultaneously. If one observes the particle's position, then one immediately affects its momentum, and if one focuses on the particle's momentum, one instantly changes its position.

So it might be with the relationship between thought and the thinking mind on one hand and one's emotive and sensorial life on the other. In other words, if one is defining one's life experiences exclusively vis-à-vis cognitive apprehensions of them, then one is inherently less attentive to the intrinsic power of one's feelings and physical reactions. Whereas, if one allows oneself on a regular basis to stay with one's feelings and sensorial reactions without trying to label or define them, or to react adversely to them due to labels and definitions, then one has a much better chance to experience them purely and directly.

At the same time, if we are to find meaning in our lives, it is necessary for us to maintain our ability to dive deeply into thoughts and words, and to understand their specific meanings as clearly as we possibly are able. Otherwise, we will inevitably tend to move farther and farther from understanding the dynamics of our world and ourselves. Therefore, how might we clearly experience the intrinsic power of feelings and sensorial reactions without diluting them with our thoughts while at the same time understanding ourselves and our world through the potential clarity which thoughts and words might bring?

Or, to stand the question on its head, how might we effectively integrate thoughts, feelings, and sensorial reactions into a larger intelligence which is capable of comprehending our world and our experiences at a deeper level than what mere cognitive apprehension of them might bring? Furthermore, where exactly might one begin in attempting to do so?

The famous Swiss psychologist Jean Piaget's theory of cognitive development, which he developed largely by observing his own children, puts forth the idea that the development of intelligence in a person is a continuous process of assimilation and accommodation. During *assimilation*, we modify or change new information we are encountering in order that it will fit into cognitive schemas with which we are already familiar. That is, we keep the new information we are encountering and add it to what already exists in our minds. Whereas, during the process of *accommodation*, we restructure those cognitive schemas so that we can effectively absorb the new information.

For example, when a child who is becoming familiar with the principle of conservation during the stage of concrete operations watches her father pour water from a large pitcher into three different glasses, she may initially believe that there is more water than before simply because it is now filling more glasses. However, if she watches her father pour the water from the glasses back into the pitcher, and it reaches the same level in the pitcher that it was at before, then the child might potentially adapt her existing cognitive schema to include the idea that the same amount of something can exist in different ways.

In terms of an adult exhibiting the same process of assimilation and accommodation, one which exists in the realm of abstract thought, someone may tend to believe that their memories of recent situations in their life, which they bring to the fore vis-à-vis their thoughts, are by and large how those situations actually occurred. That is, they rely on their thinking mind to tell them that how they remember a situation which has occurred in their recent past is either the way they remember it, or else is very close to what they remember.

However, if someone were to show them some digital film of the same situation which they were certain they remembered correctly, and it is obvious to the person that the details and dynamics of the situation are widely divergent from how they remembered them, then that person may begin to re-examine the relationship in his mind between his thoughts and his memories. Consequently, the person might then adapt his existing cognitive schemas to include the idea that the relationship in his mind between thought and memory is not as accurate as he once thought it was.

How thoughts, ideas, and memories can impede one's emotions and sensorial reactions from coming to full fruition might be better understood if the relationship between thought and memory was investigated more fully by cognitive theorists, neuroscientists, and others at the exact borderline at which thoughts turn to memories, and likewise at the point at which short-term memories become long-term ones at a place where they can be fully conceptualized.

If thoughts become solidified into memories before emotive and physical reactions can come to full fruition, then those memories might conceivably limit feelings and sensorial reactions by defining them too narrowly, thus impeding their further growth, particularly if one's thoughts have caused one's memories to be inaccurate. For the danger of memory in relation to impressionistic life is that feelings and senses will become conceptualized and then categorized before they have had enough time to reach their apex; in a sense not becoming what they were meant to be.

There is ample evidence for how our thinking minds continually change our remembrances of past experiences to the point that each time we think about a past experience we tend to change our remembrance of it. That is, as new memories of the same situation or experience continue to be made, the original memories are altered to the point where they actually cease to exist in their previous incantation. So that each time we remember something, we are moving further from our original remembrance of it.

At the same time, memory is an actual physical process, existing as subtle shifts in the strength of synaptic connections between the brain's neurons. As cells become intertwined in the brain's neuronal structure, new memories are made. In addition, our thoughts are representations of things that our brains have either perceived with our senses, felt with our emotions, or conceived of as an actual physical action (e.g., picking up the phone to call somebody). Therefore, both thought and memory are very much physical processes.

Likewise, some scientists who study thought, memory, and the brain believe that even abstract thoughts emanate from a physiological basis, putting forth the idea that abstract thoughts are essentially just "maps" (similar to the spatial map in the hippocampus region of the brain) which correspond to an individual's external environment and his or her position in it.

Eric Kandel and other neuroscientists have pointed out that in order to recognize the details of our world, our brain develops an internal representation of the world—a cognitive map—and then uses that to generate a meaningful image of what exists in the world for us to see and hear. The cognitive map is then combined with information about events in our life, and then finally our physiological reactions are used to orchestrate and determine purposeful action.

Looking at thought and memory as physical processes similar to emotions and sensorial reactions would seem to inevitably create the potential to apprehend all three as part of a larger, more integrated intelligence in which our thoughts, emotions, and senses might on occasion be effectively fused with each other as one.

Yet in order for that to occur, it would appear that a careful exploration of the fragile borderline between thought and memory would necessarily need to take place. Otherwise, the possibility might exist that memories of our past experiences, particularly inaccurate ones, might continue to impede both our emotions and sensorial reactions from coming to full fruition by limiting them within a narrow context, one that is defined by our thoughts. In so doing, not allowing us to stay with those feelings and physical sensations for as long as we might need to in order to allow them to become part of a larger, less constricting intelligence.

Examining the precarious relationship between thought and memory is obviously an endeavor which takes more than a little careful scrutiny. Primarily it involves studying how thought creates memory, and how memory can inevitably stifle creative thinking. Likewise, it involves looking at the relationship which both knowledge and rational thought might have in relation to the potentially illusory nature of both thought and memory. So this is where we will head next; to the potential, inherent boundaries of both thought and memory.

Chapter 7

Thought, Memory, Emotive, and Sensorial Experience

Most people commonly believe that their thoughts accurately describe their experiences, and that their memories are reflective of events in their lives that by and large occurred the way they remember them. That is, the supposition that both processes might be intertwined with each other as part of an illusory process is a dynamic that many people, including cognitive scientists, psychologists, and others, are often not inclined to take seriously.

Yet some who have significantly thought about and even thoroughly studied the matter have come to understand not only the limitations of thought and memory, but likewise how one of these dynamics can easily create illusions having to do with the other, particularly in terms of knowledge and past experiences.

Any number of psychologists, philosophers, and thinkers have written about how our memories of past events in our lives are largely products of our thoughts and of a thinking mind that can never create the reality of those past events exactly as we experienced them, meaning that we're forever creating vis-à-vis our memories a past that isn't entirely real. Others such as Krishnamurti have even suggested that because all knowledge is a product of the past, that too needs to be looked at with the same suspicious eye.

Of course now, due to the effects of our current digital age and how our short-term memories are under assault due to information overload, and how that impedes information which might be gathered by our short-term memory from being effectively passed on to our long-term memory, where it can be effectively stored in a manner that allows us to think intelligently about ourselves and the dynamics of our world, the relationship between thought and memory may be potentially growing ever more precarious.

In addition, as the stream of our thoughts is being continually fragmented by the jumpy, diffuse manner in which we tend to receive information on the Web, that same precarious balance between thought and memory is being further affected by the inevitable growth of a distracted awareness that is increasingly becoming part of our mental lives.

It has been known by neuroscientists for some time now that the growth and maintenance of new synaptic terminals in the brain are what produces memories. Through a complex chemical process, the synaptic changes occur in certain regions of the brain and are then perpetuated over time. At the same time, however, the brain possesses a high degree of plasticity. That is, it has a great capacity to physiologically change through both learning and experience, causing scientists to understand just how transitory and illusive changes in our physical brains brought on by thought and memory can be.

In one interesting example of brain plasticity, Susan Greenfield in *Mind Change* refers to a 2000 study by Eleanor Maguire, Professor of Cognitive Neuroscience, and a team of colleagues at University College London who studied whether or not London cab drivers would show any physical changes in their brains due to their daily experience of using their working memories to produce an internal map within themselves that would allow them to navigate London traffic more effectively.

What the researchers found in brain scans of the taxi drivers was that a particular region of the brain related to working memory, the hippocampus or spatial map, was actually bigger in the drivers than it was in others of the same age. In addition, in studying the matter further, the researchers not only discovered that having a larger hippocampus was not only what predisposed the individuals to drive cabs in the first place, but that the longer they remained cab drivers the larger their hippocampus region became.

Other examples of brain plasticity have been uncovered by APEX Brain Centers in Asheville, NC in a soldier who recovered significantly from a traumatic brain injury he sustained as a soldier fighting in the Middle East to the point that he became gainfully employed due to a brain training course; a young man struggling with learning and behavioral challenges throughout his life who was able to take and pass a GED test he wasn't able to pass previously due to a brain training program; and a young woman who suffered for years from cognitive dysfunction and an inability to read who learned to read and comprehend easily through the same training program.

If our thoughts can in fact lead to significant changes in our physiological brains, then it would appear to be not only possible, but even likely that our stored memories may not possess the same degree of clarity that many of us may have assumed they do due to the effect of our thoughts on the neuronal networks in our brains that produce those memories.

Furthermore, since our long-term memories which we use to provide ourselves with accurate accounts of our world vis-à-vis our rational mind are now being continually subjected to information overload we likewise may need to be aware of the exact ways in which our thoughts which are growing increasingly fragmented due to this overload may be changing our entirely malleable memories in a manner that gives us an incomplete account of our experiences.

Particularly now that the stream of our thoughts is being continually interrupted by how the Internet often works as an interruption machine, and how due to information overload, our memories are often being impeded from coming to full fruition, it appears to be more important than ever that we understand the dynamics of thought and memory, and in doing so attempt to potentially understand how both our emotive and sensorial responses to our world, if given a chance to do so, might be able to provide a much needed element of clarity.

The precarious boundary between thought and memory is one that is being increasingly considered with new eyes by neuroscientists, cognitive theorists, psychologists, metaphysical thinkers, and others. How do our thoughts shape our memories of past experiences? How exactly might our current digital age be shaping the neuronal pathways in our brains which pertain to thought and memory. How reliable are our working memories in this current age of information overload? And what effects do our thoughts and working memories have on our apprehension of the past, and of knowledge itself?

When we learn something new, we form connections between neurons in the brain; these synaptic connections then creating new circuits between nerve cells, in doing so essentially remapping the brain. Then, depending on how often we use what we have just learned, those synapses become either stronger or weaker. For instance, when you are recently introduced to a new person in your life, but then don't have any contact with him for the next several months, it's going to be harder to recall his name when you meet him than if you had been in contact with him several times during that same period.

The relevant question, however, in an age in which our use of the Internet and digital devices seems to be not only continually interrupting the stream of our thoughts, but is likewise playing havoc with our working memories, might be how to successfully employ both our emotive and sensorial lives in conjunction with our cognitive lives to provide us with more accurate views of ourselves and our world; in the process strengthening our intelligence through the engendering of new synaptic connections?

Recently, a "map" of emotions was discovered by the Molecular Mind Laboratory directed by neuroscientist and psychiatrist Professor Pietro Pietrini, Director of the IMT School for Advanced Studies in Lucca, Toscana, Italy. In order to investigate how the brain processes certain basic components of emotional states, Pietrini and his researchers asked a group of fifteen subjects to define and rate their emotions while watching the 1994 movie *Forrest Gump*.

In addition, the subjects were asked to report scene by scene not only their feelings, but the respective strength of those feelings on a scale from 1 to 100; those responses then being compared with twenty-five other persons who watched the same movie during a functional magnetic resonance imaging study that had been conducted in Germany.

The study revealed how emotions are represented in the brain through the existence of what the researchers termed an *emotionotopic* mapping in the right temporo-parietal territories, those associated to the complex and multifaceted emotional experience elicited by watching the movie. In summarizing their findings, Professor Pietrini and his researchers stated that they found that the activation of certain temporo-parietal brain regions can be associated with what we feel in the exact moment, thus providing us with an actual map of our emotional experiences. In addition, the IMT School study showed that various principles associated with the representation of various sensory stimuli are also responsible for the mapping of certain emotions.

Historically, emotions have often been considered by neuroscientists, psychologists, and others to be a faculty separate from cognition. That is to say, our thoughts and memories have been thought to represent different regions of our brains and psyches than that of emotive responses. However, various studies conducted recently have challenged that assumption, showing exactly how much emotive responses can actually influence what were once thought to be purely cognitive processes, such as decision-making and memory.

Psychoanalysts such as Freud have known that emotions affect cognition without the person being aware that this is happening. In his classic 1901 work, *The Psychopathology of Everyday Life*, Freud discussed how forgetting something may not just be a simple cognitive mistake but may be motivated by underlying emotional conflicts.

More recently, Nobel laureate Daniel Kahneman, the Israeli psychologist and economist notable for his work on judgment and decision-making, and his late colleague, Amos Tversky, differentiated what they termed the *cognitive unconscious* from the *dynamic unconscious;* two types of activities which take place beyond our everyday awareness. The first, activities of the cognitive unconscious, have to do with mental activities that exist beyond the influence of emotions, such as ordinary memory. The second, activities of the dynamic unconscious, have to do with the influence of emotion upon mental activities, such as when somebody forgets someone's name due to certain unconscious emotional conflicts which they have associated with that person.

Cognitive scientists have come to understand through psychoanalytic methods that not only do passions and other strong emotions affect cognition, but modern cognitive neuroscientists have likewise demonstrated neural interconnections between those areas of the brain that are active during cognition (the prefrontal cortex) and those areas of the brain that are active during emotional arousal (those in the limbic system, such as the amygdala).

Luiz Pessoa, Professor of Cognitive Science at the University of Maryland, whose interests center around interactions between cognition and emotion in the human brain, was quoted as stating in a recent research study that it is inherently problematic to divide the brain into cognitive and affective regions based on current knowledge of brain function and connectivity because the functions and neural mechanisms of cognitive processes, and the brain regions generally viewed as cognitive regions are also involved in affective processes. Therefore, each cognitive or affective region is involved in a number of different functions.

What this might mean, of course, is that areas of the mind and brain representing various emotive or sensorial responses might more easily influence purely cognitive processes than what was formerly thought to be the case. Furthermore, if this is indeed true, then it seems possible that an intelligence that was once thought to be exclusively a function of cognition might in conjunction with our thoughts and memories be part of an expanded view of intelligence that is likewise inclusive of both our feelings and our sensorial reactions.

Once again, William James and Carl Lange proposed that the conscious experience of emotion occurs only *after* the cortex region of the brain has received signals about changes in one's physiological state. So according to their model, emotions are cognitive responses to information received from bodily states determined in large part by the autonomic nervous system. That is, we feel anger toward someone *because* we recognize that we are physiologically averse to them; or we feel affection for someone only *after* our recognition that our physical body feels desire.

However, recent experimental evidence does not entirely support the James/Lange theory concerning emotion and physiology. Neuroscientist Antonio Damasio, Professor of Psychology, Philosophy, and Neurology at the University of Southern California has posited that the experience of emotion is essentially a higher order representation of a physiological reaction, and that this reaction can be both stable and persistent. As a result of his work, a consensus has been emerging for how emotions are generated through a series of specific steps: the first being an unconscious, implicit evaluation of a stimulus; the second being a physiological response; and the third being an actual conscious experience. In other words, according to this model, emotions are not necessarily cognitive responses to specific physical stimuli. Rather, they can emanate solely in the physiological realm, and then only later become defined cognitively.

The idea that our experience of an emotion begins in the physical domain, and then only later is recognized and defined in the cognitive might appear to lead to all sorts of new approaches to the possibility of a larger, holistic intelligence. For one, if our emotive reactions and physical responses indeed often originate prior to our thoughts and memories defining them, then that might suggest ways in which we can engender an intelligence in which our emotions and sensorial reactions might perceive various aspects of our world with a clarity that is sharper and more complete simply because it originates at a deeper level than that in which purely cognitive comprehensions exist.

In addition, if people grow more comfortable with experiencing their emotions and physical reactions to circumstances in their lives without having to necessarily define them with their thoughts, then that might mean that those feelings and sensorial experiences might have a better chance of coming fully to fruition simply because their germination isn't necessarily being impeded by the necessity to label them, and in doing so limiting what they might become. Consequently, the inclusion of our emotive and physical lives within the context of a larger intelligence might produce a greater level of clarity relative to perceptions of our world.

Furthermore, if emotions can be mapped in certain regions of the brain, as Professor Pietrini and his researchers found that they can, and because neuroscientists have known for some time how thoughts are similarly mapped in the hippocampus region of the brain in the spatial map, then it might be worthwhile to investigate how various experiences might lead toward thoughts and emotions being more thoroughly connected with each other in the mind and brain at not only the psychological, but also at the physiological level.

The late Robert Plutchik, who was professor emeritus at the Albert Einstein College of Medicine during much of the twentieth century, proposed what he termed a *psychoevolutionary* classification for our basic emotions in which each emotion has an evolutionary purpose which has aided in the safety and survival of both humans and animals. For instance, fear exists for purposes of protection; possessiveness exists for purposes of courtship, mating, and reproduction; sadness exists as a cry for help and potential reintegration with others; disgust exists in order to push dangerous situations away; and anticipation exists for purposes of exploration.

In other words, in the tradition of Charles Darwin and his evolutionary theory, according to Plutchik, there is a significant adaptive purpose to different emotions. That is, feelings help us humans as evolutionary members of the animal kingdom to survive and prosper by alerting us to both threats and opportunities.

Plutchik likewise proposed a model for eight basic emotions which he placed opposite each other depending upon the physiological response that each provokes; this approach being significantly different from what most researchers of emotion describe, who tend to lump emotions like fear and anger with each other simply because we often experience them together.

However, Plutchik was instead looking at physiological adaptive responses; and so he termed some such as anger and fear as being opposite to each other due to the physical response each provokes. That is, an angry person or animal tends to get loud and move toward a threatening situation or person, while a scared person or animal tends to move away from the threat.

Plutchik's ideas harken back to the evolutionary theories of Charles Darwin, who recognized that human behavior is representative of a number of emotional responses that lie between the opposing behaviors of approach and avoidance. According to Darwin, there are six universal emotions that exist on a continuum, including the two major responses of happiness and fear; the first encouraging approach while the second encourages avoidance. Between these two polar opposites, according to Darwin, are surprise, disgust, sadness, and anger. In addition, Darwin likewise postulated that some of these basic emotional responses can be combined to produce other ones, such as awe being a mixture of fear and surprise, while fear and trust can give rise to submission.

In the same vein, Rupert Sheldrake is an English author who has worked as a biochemist at Cambridge University, someone who has studied the mental life of animals for the better part of his career. His concept of *morphic resonance* posits that memory is inherent in nature and that various species inherit a collective memory from all previous members of the same species. Sheldrake claims that various perceived phenomena, particularly biological ones, become more probable the more often they occur. In other words, he proposes that newly acquired behaviors by a particular species can be automatically passed down to future members of that species, even though those behaviors may not have been directly taught to them.

That is, each individual member of a particular species draws upon and contributes to the collective memory of the species; this dynamic allowing new patterns of behavior to spread more rapidly than would otherwise be possible. For example, according to Sheldrake, there is evidence from laboratory experiments that if rats of a particular breed learn a new trick at Harvard, then rats of that same breed from all over the world are able to learn the same trick faster than they would be able to do otherwise.

If it is indeed true that our emotions, and the specific behaviors which result from them, tend to possess a deep evolutionary basis, then it might be possible that by studying certain members of the animal kingdom who evolved before human beings to better understand our own emotive lives relative to our physiological responses, and likewise relative to the clarity of our perceptions in negotiating the modern world.

Mark Bekoff, Professor Emeritus of Ecology and Evolutionary Biology at the University of Colorado, and a researcher who has studied the intelligence, emotive, and sensory lives of animals for years, alludes in a 2019 article published in *Yes!* magazine to scientific research which demonstrates that many animals are not only highly intelligent, but that they also in fact possess certain sensory and motor abilities that are far superior to ours as humans, and that they likewise possess rich emotional lives which display a wide range of emotions.

According to Bekoff, dogs are able to detect diseases such as cancer and diabetes, and likewise warn humans of impending heart attacks and strokes; elephants, whales, hippopotamuses, giraffes, and alligators use low frequency sounds to communicate over long distances; and bats, dolphins, whales, frogs, and various rodents use high-frequency sounds to find food, communicate with others, and to navigate their world.

Examples of the rich emotional life that animals possess are Bekoff's observations and accounts of magpies mourning one of their own following his death; a fox burying her fallen mate; rats, mice, and chickens displaying empathy and feeling not only their own pain, but those of other individual members of their species; elephants helping another elephant who was crippled and had trouble keeping up with the herd; a humpback whale who had gotten tangled in some crab lines doing dives and rubbing shoulders with the rescuers who had saved her as a means of thanking them; a dog running to wake up the owner of another dog after that dog's belly had become suddenly swollen following surgery; and a chimpanzee attempting to hide his embarrassment after a vine he was swinging on broke and he had fallen into a ravine.

Anyone familiar with the psychology of Carl Jung knows that Jung proposed the idea of what he called a *collective unconscious*, which he believed is a common heritage that we carry within us, in part dating back to prehuman history. He referred to the contents of the collective unconscious as *archetypes*, which in earlier versions of his theory are equivalent to instincts. According to Jung, an archetype is an unlearned tendency to experience things in a certain way.

In Jung's theory, instincts involving basic survival and reproduction are part of an archetype he called the *shadow,* which he believed derives from our prehuman, animal past, when the concerns of our evolutionary ancestors were limited to survival and reproduction, rather than being self-conscious in nature, and which we as humans still carry with us today.

One interesting example of this particular type of instinctual behavior in animals which might be seen as being carried over to human behavior would be that of the three-spined stickleback fish, a one-inch-long fish found in the rivers and lakes of Europe. During mating season, the male, normally possessing a dull coloration, becomes red and will attempt to chase away anything that is red that comes into his territory, including the reflection of a red truck in the water.

Likewise, the female undergoes a transformation as well. Normally dull in color herself, she takes on a certain silvery glow that no male stickleback can resist, and when he sees her, he swims toward her in a zigzag pattern, to which she responds by swimming toward him with her head held high. He responds by swimming toward his nest and showing her its entrance. She then enters the nest with her head sticking out at one end and her tail at the other. The male then prods at the base of her tail with rhythmic thrusts, while she releases her eggs and leaves the nest.

As one has no doubt already imagined upon reading this account of stickleback courtship, without succumbing to any sort of depraved imaginings, this particular behavior appears to be highly reminiscent of instinctual human courtship rituals. No doubt one can think of other numerous examples of these rituals which have become instinctual archetypes for we humans.

Whether we can employ the ideas of those such as Sheldrake, Bekoff, and Carl Jung to better understand not only our own evolutionary past, but likewise what we share with certain members of the animal kingdom in regard to our own emotive, sensorial, and cognitive lives remains to be seen. Yet if we can potentially use such ideas to engender a more integrated intelligence within ourselves, one in which these three aspects of our psyches might be more successfully fused because we have better understood the evolutionary histories from which each originated, this would appear to be an investigation into our psyches in conjunction with our past which might be well worth the effort.

At the same time, what needs to be studied are questions such as where exactly our sensorial lives dovetail with our emotive ones. How we can proceed with cognitive apprehensions of our world without allowing them to potentially stifle our emotive responses by defining them. Or how perceptions of events in our lives might become more immediate and direct through a fusion of cognitive, emotive, and sensorial fields.

Of course, a significant part of such an investigation into the possibility of an integrated intelligence would be looking at how we have been potentially conditioned to examine events in our lives largely through rational thought and memory, while at the same time ignoring emotive and sensorial reactions to them which might give those same events more meaning.

In addition, an important part of such an examination might be studying the precarious, often illusory dynamics of rational thought and memory in terms of that same conditioning, particularly in our current digital age, in order to see how that conditioning and those potentially illusory dynamics might impede our emotive and sensorial reactions from coming to full fruition. So this is where we will turn next; toward looking at our own conditioning and self-reflection in terms of how these might potentially affect the clarity of our perceptions of our world and ourselves.

Chapter 8

Self-Reflection and Conditioning in the Digital Age

How exactly might our current digital age be conditioning us to accept the potential limitations of both thought and memory; and how might that eventually make it more difficult for us as humans to effectively prevent those thoughts and memories from stifling our feelings and physical reactions?

We tend to assume that whenever we're considering occurrences in our lives through the dynamics of thought and memory that our thoughts and memories are actually revealing those occurrences at a point that is necessarily valid. In other words, we believe that more often than not we're able to use our memories to recall events in our lives as they in fact occurred, and that our thoughts are necessarily making significant contact with the realities which we're endeavoring to explain or clarify.

Once again, although a number of philosophers, psychologists, and others have questioned the validity of our thoughts and memories, we by and large tend to take both processes at their face value, believing them to be effective tools for navigating the circumstances of our lives. Although some have questioned the validity which we have placed on knowledge that has been accepted over the years simply because that knowledge may have emanated from the illusory dynamics of thought and memory, few have taken the time to question our belief in the role of knowledge itself in our lives.

Yet as we navigate the details of our daily lives, or as scientists and others examine whichever aspect of human knowledge has drawn their attention, our reflections about our world, whether they be the result of individual dilemmas or scientific investigations, are still most of the time the result of our thoughts and memories. At least such is the case in most of the Western world.

However, other societies in the course of human history have not relied so completely on their cognitive lives to guide them through the course of their daily lives. Dr. Joyce Frey, who holds a PhD in International Psychology from the Chicago School of Professional Psychology and has taught in various institutions over the course of her career, most recently at one in Kansas, after a meeting in the late 1980s with Russell Means, a leader in the American Indian movement, decided to immerse herself in the culture and rituals of the Cree Nation, as well as many other nations to whom the Cree introduced her.

What she found as part of her research was that the Cree and other Nations whom she observed have what she said was a "wonderful metaphysical understanding of intelligence," one in which the mind, body, and soul are all connected. Whereas, reported Dr. Frey following her research, intelligence in the Euro-Western cultures is based largely on the idea of literacy and academics, the Cree elders she spoke to viewed intelligence as being based on an understanding of nature, oral traditions, storytelling, art, and community rituals.

In other words, according to Dr. Frey's investigations of Native American cultures, their view of intelligence is more fully a part of their sensorial and emotive lives than is that of much of the Western world, where cognitive ability still largely defines what is intelligent thought and behavior.

The Seneca tribe believes that entering into silence in the mind provides a way to purify one's feelings, and that resistance to uncomfortable feelings through one's thoughts inhibits the sort of purification that would lead toward personal growth. In other words, according to the Senecas, invited thoughts that lead toward unknown fears were what prevents a growth within oneself that creates a balance between self and nature, between social and physical environments, and likewise prevents a realm of individual existence from flourishing in which self-satisfaction is earned. In other words, in the eyes of the Seneca tribe, the cognitive life plays a significantly lesser part in promoting human intelligence than it does in our current Western world.

As one can imagine, there are other cultures, particularly non-Western ones, where greater value is placed on the social and emotional aspects of intelligent behavior (particularly where those noncognitive skills are closely tied to a successful life). For instance, in Zimbabwe, Africa, caring for relatives over friends or strangers is considered to be a higher form of intelligence. In addition, researchers working with Zimbabwe children found that although the children struggled with traditionally expressing themselves using pen and paper, they were particularly talented clay-molders.

Dr. Robert Serpell, who returned recently to the University of Zambia after spending thirteen years at the University of Maryland, and who has studied concepts of intelligence in rural African communities since the 1970s, has found that people in some African communities—particularly those in which Western schooling has not become common—tend to blur the line between intelligence and social competence more than people living in Western societies do.

For instance, Dr. Serpell found that in rural Zambia, the concept of what people there refer to as intelligence (*nzelu*) includes both cleverness (*chenjela*) and responsibility (*tumikila*); so when Zambian parents discuss the intelligence of their children, they prefer not to separate the purely cognitive aspect of intelligence from the social responsibility aspect.

During the past several years, American Psychological Association President Dr. Robert J. Sternberg of Yale University, and Dr. Elena Grigorenko, director of the Center for the Psychology of Abilities at Yale, while investigating concepts of intelligence among the *Luo* people in Kenya, found that intelligence to them consists of not only Western ideas of academic intelligence, but also includes social qualities like respect, responsibility, and consideration, in addition to skills like practical thinking or comprehension. In another study of the *Luo*, Dr. Sternberg found that children who score high on a test of knowledge about medicinal herbs—a measure of practical intelligence—tend to score poorly on tests of academic intelligence.

The results of Sternberg and Grigorenko, published in the journal *Intelligence*, suggest that practical and academic intelligence can develop independently or even in conflict with each other. The two researchers also agree with studies which have taken place in other countries which suggest that people who are unable to solve complex problems abstractly can often solve them when they are presented in a more familiar societal context.

Of course, the next obvious question relative to the development of a more holistic intelligence is what we might be able to learn from other societies and their views on intelligent thought and behavior so that we might not only view the idea of intelligence within our own society from a broader perspective, but likewise fuse those other views with our own more limited view of intelligence, one that is often heavily reliant on rational thought, memory, and knowledge that is apprehended primarily cognitively.

For instance, could the specific skills of the *Luo* people in regard to social qualities like respect, responsibility, and consideration become effectively fused with Howard Gardner's interpersonal or intrapersonal types of intelligence; or could their emphasis on becoming familiar with certain qualities which medicinal herbs possess be used to clarify what his naturalist intelligence represents?

Likewise, could the manner in which parents in Zambia prefer not to separate purely cognitive intelligence in their children from the idea of social responsibility be used by Westerners to expand on the ideas of developmental psychologists in regard to how cognitive development might be fused with psychosocial development to provide a larger view of how and when specific stages of developmental growth take place?

In similar ways, by studying the view of intelligence that the Cree Indians espouse, one in which mind, body, and spirit are all connected, we might be able to develop a clearer idea of what exactly the limitations of our thoughts and memories might be. Or in carefully examining what the Seneca mean when they speak of how we might be able to purify our minds by dropping our natural resistance to uncomfortable thoughts, those of us in the Western world may become more prone to think in terms of using an investigation into the conflicts inherent in the structure of our thinking minds and into the process of thought itself to probe a larger intelligence which may lay on the other side of thought and memory.

Yet to begin to access that larger intelligence, it seems necessary to first examine exactly how we are conditioned to believe that our thoughts and memories rest on the sort of firm base that we tend to believe they do. In other words, how representative are they of the actual dynamics of the world in which we live?

Once again, David Bohm, in his book *Wholeness and the Implicate Order,* makes mention of how our particular systems of thought and language can prevent us from observing the details and dynamics of our world from a larger perspective. Referencing Piaget's ideas on how the process of assimilation and accommodation works in the development of cognitive structures, that which might allow one to perceive his or her world from a point of heightened intelligence, Bohm makes the point that in developing a newer, clearer perception of one's world, one must necessarily begin by observing the new fact or dynamic which one is attempting to assimilate in what he calls its *full individuality*, and from there create the order within oneself that is conducive to comprehending the particular fact or dynamic.

In other words, one does not begin with an abstract preconception of what one is observing, and from there attempt to adapt that particular abstraction to a new fact or dynamic in order to properly understand it. Instead, one works from a point of view in which one's abstract conceptions of the world are made to conform to the particular dynamics of whatever new fact one is attempting to assimilate.

For example, in attempting to comprehend relativity theory, Einstein, after initially beginning with the fact that light always travels at a constant speed and that occurrences should be seen as being the same by two observers regardless of their positions relative to each other, initially considered how those two opposing realities might be fused with each other to produce a larger theory.

Instead, however, what he eventually did was to make his theory of gravitation conform to the impossibility of assimilating the constancy of light speed into what had been standard relativity theory to produce his brilliant theory of special relativity in which Isaac Newton's previous idea of absolute time was finally dismissed.

Likewise, Pablo Picasso, after first attempting to create a conception of how he might present the same subject in one of his paintings from multiple perspectives through the use of standard three-dimensional space, eventually made his ideas on space and perspective conform to Henri Poincare's ideas concerning the possibility of a four-dimensional space, and in doing so was able to geometrize space through a multiplicity of different viewpoints in creating the brilliant paintings that followed.

In other words, it was Picasso's willingness to abandon his initial ideas on how to use three-dimensional space to present a single subject from multiple perspective for something entirely new—a four-dimensional

space—that allowed his abstract conceptions concerning space and perspective to adapt themselves to a newer, more workable reality.

The difference between these two approaches to assimilating information from the world creatively is particularly profound for a couple
of important reasons. On the one hand, if one begins with a preconceived idea concerning a particular piece of information or relevant
dynamic concerning whatever one is investigating and then attempts
to make those things fit one's abstract preconceptions, then one is not
really in touch with whatever one is examining. Rather, one is simply
attempting to make the relevant information, facts, or dynamics fit what
one already knows. In other words, one remains a step or two away
from being fully connected to whatever has drawn one's interest.

On the other hand, before formulating any abstract conceptions concerning the area which one is investigating, one instead allows oneself
to simply look in detail at whatever one is attempting to understand,
particularly those things which at first might not seem to be able to
co-exist with each other, and then attempts to sit with whatever one
has discovered with the sort of purity of mind which has dropped all
resistance to uncomfortable, conflicting thoughts, that which the Seneca
Indians believed would help them to better understand their world, then
one is fully connected to whatever he or she is investigating.

In terms of a potential attempt to formulate an integrated, holistic
intelligence in which cognitive, emotive, and sensorial reactions are
fused to produce moments of clear, direct insight—the *aha* moment of
creative absorption—the distinction between these two approaches to
investigating one's world would appear to be highly important, particularly in terms of allowing emotive and sensorial reactions to come to
full fruition before attempting to fuse them with cognitive ones.

Needless to say, it has become almost a habitual part of our individual
existences to attempt to define whatever emotions or physical reactions
we are experiencing before allowing ourselves to experience them at
a place that exists beyond words, thoughts, or ideas. For instance, one
experiences a certain amount of anxiety in terms of a particular situation in one's life, such as in meeting someone with whom they have
had conflicted relations in the past but haven't seen in a while. So one
inevitably engages in things such as attempting to squelch a certain
amount of anxiety by mentally controlling it through past justifications
for one's behavior; replaying past experiences with the person in one's

mind in order to give oneself more confidence before meeting them; or else trying to discover the exact source of one's anxiety.

However, even though most of us have been heavily conditioned to try to control negative emotions through the use of our cognitive apprehensions of them, if instead one simply sits with his or her feeling of anxiety while letting it grow until it comes to full fruition without attempting to define, rationalize, or suppress it, then after one has allowed this full blooming of the feeling of anxiety to occur, one might be able to use one's thoughts and memories to better understand what is occurring within oneself.

Likewise, in that moment, there is a distinct possibility that feelings and physical reactions to the person one is anxious about meeting, when effectively fused together because they have been allowed to come to fruition, might lead toward a moment of genuine insight in which one is able to meet the particular person in an intelligent manner simply because one has been able to fully connect to the particular situation, and thus see it and the person more clearly.

Nearly all of us who have come of age in the Western world have been conditioned to believe that we necessarily need to depend on our thinking minds to clarify the dynamics of our world for us; whether it be in terms of personal situations, explorations of our immediate environment, or even in terms of attempting to find some larger meaning to our individual existences.

At the same time, however, because our thoughts concerning various situations in our lives are often so heavily based on our memories of previous situations, it may often be the case that what we are experiencing with our feelings or physical reactions is often being defined by us relative to what we have experienced in the past, rather than what we are apprehending in the immediate present. Consequently, that explanation of what we have experienced in the past might easily serve to prevent us from being fully in touch with what we are experiencing in the present.

In other words, if people were more willing to stay with their immediate impressions of whatever they are experiencing in the present moment until these have come to full fruition, and then only use their thinking minds to clarify for themselves what they have just experienced they would most likely be more directly in touch with the essential dynamics of their world.

Unfortunately, this is most often not the case, particularly when it comes to explorations of our world in search of something new or different. That is, when searching for answers which will help to clarify the many different aspects of life in the world through some sort of original apprehension of them, often before we even realize what is occurring within ourselves, we have begun to use rational thought and memory, both of which significantly involve apprehending one's world vis-à-vis past experiences, to provide us with some new way of looking at circumstances that we do not yet fully comprehend.

Particularly this is the case in terms of how children in their formative years are taught in the vast majority of schools today in our society. Rather than allowing them to fully experience something new about which they are learning, teachers tend to immediately apply cognitive apprehensions of the material to the lesson before their students have been able to connect with it by using the full power of their impressions.

For example, children in a middle-school science class may be looking at various slides of microorganisms under a microscope. What often occurs in most classrooms is that their teacher will begin introducing them to processes of naming and classification before the students have been able to experience the full power of their impressions of the small creatures at which they are looking. Consequently, their cognitive processes of naming and classification might easily begin to overwhelm how the microorganisms are affecting them at an emotive or sensorial level.

For those who would make the argument that the children might still be able to fully experience their impressions in regard to the microscopic life forms they are studying while still using their cognitive processes to classify and name them, those people should bear in mind that when someone, particularly a child, must necessarily leave impressionistic, absorbing experience to focus on cognitive processes such as memorization, classification, or any other linear sequence of purely cerebral activities, then his or her primary focus tends to become one of thought processes rather than that of vivid impressions.

Therefore, it would appear to be important that teachers of students in their formative years make sure to provide them with enough time to become fully acquainted with whatever sensorial or emotive impressions they are experiencing so that their impressionistic lives might grow to full fruition, and so that eventually as they grow toward adulthood their emotive and sensorial existences have the opportunity to become fully fused into a larger, more integrated intelligence.

Lately, the idea of *embodied cognition* has been receiving significant attention from the scientific community; this being defined as the way in which our bodies interact with the world shapes the way we think. In other words, the mind is not only connected to the body, but the body influences the mind. For example, according to this theory, if participants in a study are told to make an effort to grimace and frown, they will then be able to comprehend dramatically dark sentences faster than they will joyful, pleasant ones.

In one 2011 experiment researchers had undergraduate students estimate how tall certain objects like the Eiffel Tower were, looking at pictures of the objects while standing on a balance board. During the experiment the researchers shifted slightly the balance of the participants on the board so that they were unaware that their posture was shifting. What the researchers found was that the participants' posture actually affected how tall they believed the Eiffel Tower to be. That is, the researchers found that leaning slightly left caused the subjects to believe the tower was smaller than how they would have perceived it if they were standing on a flat surface.

In 1992, researchers Francisco Varela, Evan Thompson, and Eleanor Rosch introduced in their iconic book *The Embodied Mind: Cognitive Science and Human Experience* the concept of *enaction* in order to place emphasis on the idea that the experienced world is portrayed and determined by mutual interactions between the physiology of the organism, its sensorimotor circuits, and its environment.

One implication of their view is that only a creature with particular features—e.g., eyes, hands, legs, and certain motor skills—can possess certain kinds of cognitive capacities because the world that is experienced by one is not only conditioned by the neural activity of the person's brain, but in fact emerges through the bodily activities of the organism; the three researchers arguing that the standard division between external features of the world and internal symbolic representations within a person's mind should be dispensed with as it is unable to explain the effect of embodied, physical activities on cognition.

In conjunction with the idea of embodied cognition is the concept of *interoception*: our brain's representation of sensations from our body. According to Lisa Feldman Barrett, professor at Northeastern

University and President of the Association for Psychological Science, our brains didn't necessarily evolve for us to think and perceive the world accurately; nor did they even really evolve so that we could see, hear, or feel. They evolved in order to regulate our bodies so that we could move around in the world more efficiently.

Because the core task of a brain working in service to a body, when looked at in this manner, is to regulate the body's systems through the anticipation of needs and the preparation to satisfy them before they arise, the consequence of this sensory activity is central to everything from thought, to emotion, to decision making, to sense of self. In fact, Barrett has said that because our body is part of our mind in a very biological way, this means that there is a piece of our body in every concept that we form, even in term of thoughts that we tend to believe are entirely cognitive in nature.

In addition, Barrett believes that in order to maintain this process of equilibrium between mind and body, the brain must continually form concepts that guide the body by integrating pieces of sensory input with memories of similar experiences from the past; thus allowing the brain to infer the causes of sensory information that it receives through the eyes or other sensory organs. Consequently, according to Barrett, this predictive process allows us to navigate the details of our world, guide our actions, and intelligently construct our experiences by forming reasonable concepts about them as they occur.

For example, a person may be walking through a certain neighborhood in a large city and while doing so experiences a sudden rapid heartbeat and a rigidity in their muscles without initially knowing the exact cause of these particular physical sensations. In becoming aware of them, the person begins to take note of the racial composition of the neighborhood which they are negotiating, seeing that it contains a large number of persons of a certain ethnic minority. Making an immediate connection between their sudden rapid heartbeat and the rigidity in their muscles and the neighborhood which they are now traversing, individuals are able to recognize within themselves a certain biased aversion toward specific minorities of which they hadn't previously been aware.

At its most basic level interoception, according to those who have studied the idea, allows us to determine how we feel at any particular moment through awareness of various physical sensations such as a growling stomach or a racing heart. As a result of this sensorial awareness, we're then able to more effectively experience essential emotions like anxiety, sadness, or frustration. Consequently, we're able to manage the way we feel by taking the appropriate action based on the body's signals of which we've become aware.

Obviously, the ideas of embodied cognition and interoception are closely related; the first proposing that the way our bodies interact with the world shapes the way we think, the second having to do with how we can use our awareness of our body's reactions to develop appropriate emotions and reactions to circumstances in our life. Both have to do with using our awareness of our body's physical reactions to the world to develop appropriate reactions to events in our life.

Of course, a question looming over all of this in terms of learning what our sensorial, emotive, and physical reactions might be able to teach us concerning the development of the power of direct insight, one which allows us to confront the details and circumstances of our lives in searching for an intelligence which might exist beyond the bounds of thought and memory, is what exactly the nature of this more expansive intelligence might be and how exactly one might proceed in attempting to apprehend it.

Quite possibly part of that answer may lay in an examination of the potential relationship which might exist between an enriched sensorial and/or emotive life and our capacity to closely attend to the dynamics of our world to the point where our observations of our world and what we are observing might become one and the same; a place where the psychological space between these two things might begin to disappear. More specifically, what might the work of certain great artists and visionaries be able to teach us about this concern, particularly in terms of their extreme attention to both the details of their world and likewise what is occurring within themselves? Therefore, this is where we will journey next, into the world of important creators and visionaries, and coincidentally into the relationship which might exist between one's capacity to attend and the richness of their inner life.

Chapter 9

An Enriched Intelligence

The great nineteenth century naturalist and writer of the iconic book *Walden*, Henry David Thoreau, faced an intense personal crisis as a young man when his beloved brother John died suddenly from neurotoxins which were released into his body during a tetanus infection which began after he accidentally cut off the tip of his finger while shaving. After replacing part of the missing finger and wrapping it with a bandage, he began suffering from lockjaw, with his body becoming stiff as a board. After suffering days of violent spasms with his body aching intensely, John died in Henry's arms.

In grieving for his dead brother during the ensuing days, Thoreau then suffered what today might be called PTSD (Post Traumatic Stress Disorder), even strangely enough succumbing to his own form of lockjaw in which he endured the same skeleton-tightening muscle spasms that had caused his brother's death to become so horrific for him.

In reaction to this, while living at the edge of Walden Pond amidst a beautiful natural setting and isolating himself from the travails of human society, he composed *A Week on the Concord and Merrimack Rivers* as a memorial of sorts to his dead brother, an activity which today might well be categorized as an example of PTG (Post Traumatic Growth), which those who have studied the matter would define as positive changes that occur as the result of one's struggles with highly challenging life crises.

In other words, in writing his now famous essay, Thoreau was performing the sort of cognitive and emotive work which psychologists say occurs as the result of productive ruminations which can take place when there is enough distance between oneself and a traumatic event so as not to cause undue emotional distress.

No doubt his famous quote, *"Most men live lives of quiet despera-tion,"* which he wrote in his follow-up book *Walden,* came about as the result of his endeavor to develop a perception of the possibilities which his own life might represent in comparison with the masses of other men, and which no doubt led to his decision to embrace his own version of solitude during his two-year sojourn communing with nature at Walden Pond.

There he was able to attend to and lose himself in the details of the natural world in which he found himself, from specific bird calls and animal sounds to different types of wildflowers; to experiencing a school of small perch suddenly rise to the surface of the pond and leave bubbles on it while he watched the seemingly bottomless water into which they descended reflect clouds overhead as he experienced himself floating through the air as in a balloon; to watching leaves, twigs, stones, and cobweb all sparkle in the midafternoon sun as if they were covered with dew during a spring morning—a world which he described as being pristine and otherworldly.

Likewise, Ludwig van Beethoven composed his iconic otherworldly *Ninth Symphony* during the early nineteenth century as he was losing his hearing in its entirety, and so was dealing with the despair which surely followed as he realized that he had lost the one faculty that was most important to him, both as a composer and as a human being. The symphony, which many have categorized as the expression of a revo-lutionary optimism, can be heard as the voice of a man who refuses to bow to adversity, who passes through the darkest of nights and emerges triumphant.

Despite his increasing deafness, Beethoven was still able for years to compose music of the highest quality by inwardly hearing in his head the incredible music he was creating. At the same time, however, his deafness meant that he struggled to conduct the very music he had composed, often falling out of time with the orchestra who was playing it. After being significantly ridiculed by the public for this, he withdrew more and more into his own private world where eventually he com-posed his iconic *Ninth Symphony*.

At the time he conducted the symphony's initial performance he was entirely deaf, and so appeared on the podium in a disheveled, unkempt state, unable to keep the correct time to his own symphony and even continued to furiously wave his arms in the air even after the orchestra had stopped playing it.

Yet like Thoreau, Beethoven was able to use the trauma he experienced in losing his hearing in uniting it with both his deep impressionistic life and his brilliant cognitive ability to compose a work for a full symphony orchestra during a similar period of posttraumatic growth. In fact, almost certainly without passing through the dark night of the soul he must have experienced as he was growing deaf, he would not have been able to come out the other side of it, so to speak, in composing his defiantly optimistic *Ninth Symphony*.

What the life stories of these two men represent is that of someone using the sort of deep pain they have experienced to create something entirely new, using all their human faculties to do so while diving deeply into their emotive and sensorial lives, and then coming out the other side with an entirely original vision. In both situations, the entire process was that of great artists fusing challenging emotive experience with deeply sensorial experience (Beethoven's intensely dramatic approach to music and Thoreau's otherworldly love of nature) in creating a vision having very much to do with their extraordinary abilities (Beethoven's as a composer and Thoreau's as a writer describing the natural world).

In both cases the depth of each man's pain assisted him in creating a unique experience born of that pain which then allowed him to tap into a particular transcendent, original view of his world. Furthermore, it is simply not possible to separate their emotive pain from their heightened sensorial experience, or for that matter from the clarity of their unique vision.

At the same time, the fact that neither Thoreau nor Beethoven had a sexual life of any genuine consequence speaks of an intensity of a spiritual life that could almost be described as erotic in nature. Thoreau's passionate love of the natural world which provided him with endless opportunities for an experience of its sights, sounds, smells, colors, and other details which could almost be described as otherworldly; and Beethoven's expression of a purity of heart which was on full display in his magnificent Pastoral Symphony and in the exquisite, shy tenderness which was part of his iconic Moonlight Sonata speak of a consciousness which has found something much deeper than mere romantic love.

There is of course also the matter of attention; the degree to which great artists like Thoreau and Beethoven were able to fully attend to what was taking place within them relative to what they were endeavoring to create, and what we can learn from Thoreau's ability to attend to his natural surroundings so intently over such a long period time, and likewise from Beethoven's capacity to focus so fully on the revolutionary music he was hearing in his head even after he had lost his hearing.

Furthermore, what might we, even though many of us of course may not have the same creative vision as a Thoreau or a Beethoven, be able to learn relative to the search for a larger, integrated intelligence born of an increased capacity to attend to our inner lives, and in so doing fuse them with the dynamics of our outer world? Indeed, this question might be relevant in our current digital age that so many who have studied the matter say is adversely affecting our capacity to attend as we jump relentlessly from one link or one website to the next.

This question of course is inextricably related to the degree to which the depth of our impressions affects our ability to become absorbed in both our own inner world and likewise in the details and dynamics of our outer world. Almost certainly, the richer and more fulfilling the first is the more potentially successful the second endeavor becomes. Thoreau was able to lose himself so completely in the natural world he experienced at Walden Pond due to his heightened sensorial life; and Beethoven was able to immerse himself so completely within the iconic music he was creating because of the depth of his emotive life.

Previously, many neuroscientists, psychologists, and others have regarded attention essentially as a function of cognition. That is, one's ability to focus clearly on the details of one's world or on the dynamics taking place within oneself have been regarded as primarily mental activities related to faculties like concentration, or on the ability to avoid distraction whenever necessary. Yet, in carefully studying the work of any number of great artists and visionaries, it soon becomes obvious that their ability to remain absorbed in what they were creating was integrally a part of their emotive and sensorial lives. In fact, one might even make the supposition that the capacity to focus and attend and the depth of one's inner life are inextricably bound together.

In studying the dynamics of attention, it would appear necessary to look at the essential difference between the activity of attention and that of concentration; in so doing regarding them as essentially different processes. Concentration of course has to do with limiting one's field of perception in order to remain attentive to whatever one is endeavoring to focus upon, and in so doing blocking out anything which might distract one from the details of that focus. In other words, concentration always involves this limiting aspect of perception, that which endeavors to ferret out possible irrelevant information which might impede the most intense concentration.

Attention, on the other hand, if it is to remain true to its essential nature, always involves the attempt to expand one's field of perception to the greatest degree possible without losing focus. Rather than being the sort of reducing valve that it is usually seen as, one that serves to eliminate potential irrelevances so that someone can instead focus on what is most essential in any circumstance or situation, it attempts to take in as much of an entire field of perception as it can absorb without losing the critical ability to focus.

Yet because we have been so conditioned to regard attention and concentration as being one and the same, we tend to believe that in order to pay attention to something, we invariably need to eliminate many of the details of what we are attempting to apprehend, and instead direct our attention to only either a singular detail or at most only a few details of whatever situation we are endeavoring to understand.

As Aldous Huxley put it in *The Doors of Perception*, for us as human beings to biologically survive in the world by differentiating between relevant and irrelevant sensory information, and in so doing focusing on what is most important, what might become a mind that is exponentially more expansive is instead often inevitably narrowed as information becomes funneled through the brain and central nervous system. Consequently, what appears to us when we attend to the details of our world is often only a measly trickle of the kind of larger consciousness which might be otherwise available.

Therefore, what exactly will allow us to expand the field of our awareness without losing the ability to focus? At the same time, what will allow our impressions of our world to become intensified and enriched without us losing perspective on what we are perceiving? And how might those two capacities—expanded awareness and deeper impressions—become fused in a way in which our ability to attend is not only not diminished, but is in fact strengthened?

These two questions are inevitably at the heart of asking if there is in fact a more expansive intelligence on the other side of thought and memory that we can access through a larger field of attention existing beyond concentration which at the same time deepens our impressions of whatever we are perceiving.

Certainly, the depth of our emotive and sensorial lives is critical to our ability to attend to the details of our world. That is, the more immersed we become in what we are feeling and what we are experiencing with our senses the greater the possibility becomes that we will be able to become fully absorbed in the details and dynamics of the world that we inhabit.

Yet at the same time, for this heightened state of impressionistic attention to exist it would appear to be critically important that there are no barriers, either intrinsic or extrinsic, conscious or unconscious, preventing us from becoming fully immersed in whatever aspects of our world we are endeavoring to attend.

As has been previously mentioned in this work, although most of us don't realize the possibility of this, the observer and the observed might on occasion become one and the same. That is to say, whatever we are observing or experiencing during any particular moment in our lives might in fact be what we *are*, rather than being something that is separate from our inner life. Yet because we have separated in our minds observer and observed, experiencer and experienced, from each other, this separation has become a significant intrinsic barrier to becoming fully immersed in the details and dynamics of our world as we continue to hold them at arm's length.

Occasionally some visionary thinker or artist like Thoreau or Beethoven is able to break through the self-imposed intrinsic barrier between experiencer and experienced to become fully immersed in a new world of creative absorption, but for most of us the observer and the observed still exist as fundamentally separate entities. As a result, a world of expanded attention and complete immersion remains for the most part fundamentally unavailable to most of us.

Although it may be given attention by certain visionaries and artists, the idea that we might have true insight into our world by becoming fully immersed in its details and dynamics without necessarily having to understand them from a cognitive viewpoint is still not on most people's radar screens even as our current digital age is now having such a profound effect on our attention spans, working memories, and the stream of our thoughts.

The relevant question of course is: Is there an insight born solely of emotion or sensorial experience, or is it necessary that cognition becomes part of such an insight in order that it be understood? That is, do we need to use our thoughts and memories to fully understand what we have just experienced with our emotions and physiological responses to events in our lives, or is there a way to correctly apprehend our world on the other side of thought and memory, using only our feelings and sensorial reactions while dispensing with cognitive apprehensions when they are not needed?

To put the matter even more succinctly, is there an insight that takes place beyond the bounds of thought and memory, yet at the same time remains entirely comprehensible to the person experiencing the insight? Furthermore, to properly examine this question, it would appear to be necessary to understand how much of emotive experience takes place at the conscious level, and how much of it is unconscious experience?

Otherwise, if a significant amount of emotive experience exists at an unconscious level, then it seemingly becomes more difficult for it to become part of a larger intelligence in which it is fused with that *aha* moment of creative absorption, simply because that moment of insight if it is to become meaningful necessarily implies that it emanate from conscious experience.

In his iconic book on insight, Eric Kandel asked the question if conscious and unconscious emotions are represented differently in the brain, and do they have different ways of expressing themselves in the body? In answering it, he wrote of how until the end of the nineteenth century, the origination of emotion was thought to consist of a particular sequence of events.

That is, a certain event, be it frightening or pleasurable, is recognized cognitively in the brain's cerebral cortex region of the person who experiences it. Then, in response to this cognitive recognition, unconscious changes are produced in the body's autonomic nervous system, leading to increased heart rate, increased blood pressure, moist palms, and the like. In other words, according to this theory, the cognitive experience of emotion was thought to take place before the body's physiological response.

However, as was discussed earlier, William James had the important insight that conscious experience of emotion only takes place *after* the body's physical response to an occurrence. In other words, we first process a strong emotional stimulus physically through bodily events like increased heart rate and rapid breathing, and then consequently we process what we are feeling through thoughts, ideas, and memories that explain the physiological changes that are taking place within us. In other words, it is the physiological changes taking place in us that allow us to experience emotion; and that without them emotions would be experienced only as sterile, disembodied entities.

Consequently, if there is indeed an intelligence on the other side of thought and memory, one in which a direct insight into the events of one's life takes place during moments of creative absorption, then emotive experience needs to be a conscious part of this process so that it can be successful fused with both sensorial experience and cognitive understanding. This then, of course, begs the question of how to engender a greater awareness in people into the origination of their emotions so that these don't remain often unconscious.

If emotions do indeed possess a physiological basis, then that would appear to lead toward an examination of how bodily reactions to occurrences in one's life lead toward moments of direct insight. For instance, what might have been occurring sensorially with Beethoven while he was composing his iconic, otherworldly *Ninth Symphony*; and correspondingly, what might have been transpiring within Thoreau's sensorial life to cause him to become so acutely aware of what the natural world might be able to teach him?

In addition, this would appear to be a significant difference between purely cerebral, cognitive intelligence and direct insight. The first is fundamentally separate from sensorial, bodily reactions to occurrences in one's life, while the second originates in the world of physiology, even though thought and memory often serve to eventually clarify for one the meaning of those moments of pure insight.

Yet intelligence is still largely defined today by either the knowledge or information which one possesses in their working memory, or how facile they are at using their rational thought processes to come to a moment of clarification. Certainly, many of us know people who have a storeroom of knowledge at their fingertips or can explain some phenomenon with a stark clarity in purely rational terms. Yet, at the same time, there often appears to be something missing relative to their overall level of intelligence; this likely being the absence of insight that originates with an enriched sensorial or emotive life.

The great essayist Susan Sontag in her insightful, essay from 1965, *Against Interpretation*, argued that rather than indulge in endless interpretations of what a certain work of art means, we need instead to recover our senses; to *see* more, *hear* more, and *feel* more. In other words, as she put it, our task in apprehending great art is not to find the maximum amount of content, and likewise not attempt to squeeze more content out of the work than is already there. Rather, our task should be to cut back on an interpretation of what a specific work of art means so that we can experience exactly *what it is* more directly and clearly. Consequently, her now famous statement which she included at the end of her essay was: "In place of a hermeneutics of art, we need an erotics of art."

In reading Sontag's iconic essay, it would appear to be true that what we need, in addition to a means of apprehending great art, and likewise in order to become more familiar with the details of our life with our senses and emotions, is some means of looking at intelligence as direct insight, rather than simply as a cognitive activity having to do primarily with rational thought or memory; this need being increasingly necessary in our present digital age when the stream of our thoughts, our working memories, and our capacity to focus and attend are now under assault by how people are obsessively using their digital devices.

Yet in order to probe this more expansive view of what intelligence seen as direct insight might entail, it would appear that we need to begin with the latter and then work our way back in search of how it relates to the former. In other words, how might an insight in which our impressionistic reactions to the world are predominate allow us to perceive our world more clearly before reacting to it more intelligently?

In the same vein, we might even be bold enough to ask the question of how much of our rational thought processes and working memories might we be able to dispense with in our current digital age in order to see the world more clearly and in so doing react to it out of genuine insight rather than out of a more limiting cognitive apprehension? However, to answer that question, it seems important that we first closely examine the essential difference between intelligent thought and direct insight.

Chapter 10

Intelligence and Insight

If one were to attempt to define how the processes of rational thought and direct insight differ from each other, one might do well to start by describing the former as a top-down process in which the mind and brain attempt to conceptualize information and knowledge in order to better understand them, while one might describe creative absorption and direct insight as processes that take place from the bottom up, those which depend largely on signals given to us by our sensorial and emotive experience.

Of course, it is the confluence of these two processes which eventually can turn insight into intelligent action, particularly if they exist simultaneously as part of a larger, more integrated intelligence. However, at the same time, if one is to comprehend exactly how such a larger intelligence might take place, it seems critically important to carefully examine how the top-down nature of intelligent thought and the bottom-up nature of direct insight actually occur. Otherwise, there might be confusion as to how the two of them might become fully integrated with each other into something larger.

Once again, a significant part of cognition involves conceptualizing information for purposes of clarity. In other words, abstract thought and the ability to manipulate various concepts have always been key components of cognitive intelligence relative to how one comprehends the dynamics and details of the world in which he or she lives. In terms of cognitive development, we know that the development of a child's intelligence is a steady progression from concrete mental operations toward the capacity for abstract thought.

On the other hand, the bottom-up nature of a direct insight into the details and dynamics of one's world, that which often occurs beyond the inevitable barriers of thought and memory, takes place via how thoroughly we might become absorbed in the emotive and sensorial experience that is provided us by the world in which we live. Just as the ability to conceptualize occurrences vis-à-vis rational thought is fundamental to cognitive intelligence, the capacity to sink fully into feelings, sensorial experience, and visual perception is critical to how a direct insight born of creative absorption might take place.

Naturally, a fundamental concern as far as both cognitive intelligence and direct insight is an examination of how and where these two processes might not just touch each other, but in fact become fully integrated into a larger, more expansive consciousness. In other words, questions need to be asked such as how exactly might cognitive apprehension and expansive emotional experience be fused with one another to produce moments of insight? How might significant visual experience be used to look critically at the limitations of thought and memory? Or where is the exact point where thought and memory begin to interfere with a direct insight achieved through a complete sensorial or emotive absorption in one's world?

These are questions not just for neuroscientists and cognitive psychologists, but likewise for those thinkers who have taken time to explore the metaphysical realm where the search for a larger consciousness becomes paramount. In fact, without both types of experts taking time to carefully explore the world of the other, it becomes difficult to see just how the above questions might ever be successfully addressed.

That is, without an examination of what an expansive consciousness might entail, neuroscientists and experts in cognition might find it difficult to fuse cognition with emotive and perceptual experience simply because they would inevitably find it difficult to put themselves in touch with the sort of larger intelligence toward which the fusion of these two worlds might lead. Conversely, without the assistance of neuroscientists and cognitions, and the scientific expertise which they bring, this search for a larger intelligence might easily devolve into abstract speculations that are not solidly grounded in human experience.

Recently, E. O. Wilson, the American biologist, naturalist, and renowned entomologist who is considered by many to be the most important living biologist in the world, published his latest book, *The Origins of Creativity,* in which he proposes that the next generation of great minds explore the symmetry between the natural sciences and the humanities; urging a refocus on philosophy in an era in which, according to him, societies who are drowning in information are starved for wisdom.

During a 2018 interview in the *Harvard Gazette*, he was asked to consider the question if since scientific investigation is a product of the human brain, can science actually exist outside of human consciousness? Wilson's answer was that yes, if one is willing to delete the word "human," science exists wherever intelligent life has evolved. In other words, scientific principles can in fact exist anywhere even if they are unable to be detected or seen by humans.

For instance, the scientific principles which Einstein eventually employed to develop his relativity theory actually existed in the universe long before there were people on earth to discover them. In the same manner, the scientific principles upon which Charles Darwin relied to prove his evolutionary theory existed long before there were people on earth, such as Darwin, to uncover them in the different species of the animal kingdom.

Therefore, what seems particularly prescient relative to the questions asked in this particular work concerning the potential evolution of a larger, more integrated intelligence is Wilson's visionary suggestion that scientific investigation can exist anywhere where intelligent life has evolved, and not necessarily exclusively within the field of human consciousness. Of course, this naturally begs the question of what exactly does a science outside the parameters of human consciousness actually entail, and how might it in fact operate? In addition, how might such a potential science beyond human consciousness be properly apprehended?

In addition, might human beings have the capacity to proceed with scientific investigations into their world solely through moments of direct insight and creative absorption, without needing to necessarily employ a scientific method based largely on rational thought and past knowledge?

The scientific method, as many of us know, involves a series of fundamental steps in investigating the details and dynamics of one's world. Essentially, they involve careful observation of a particular phenomenon or series of phenomena; formulation of a hypothesis based on inductive reasoning which might explain those observations; experimental and measurement-based testing of one's hypothesis; and then, finally, the formulation of a theory derived from those experimental findings.

In other words, the entire process is in fact a movement from questioning and uncertainty concerning what one has observed toward increasing certainty relative to potentially new knowledge. In addition, as part of this process, formulation of original ideas relative to what one has observed have to be scientifically verified before they can be taken seriously, and then turned into an actual workable theory.

However, a larger question relative to the idea that moments of direct insight might be able to occasionally replace this method of investigating one's world would appear to be one of asking what exactly constitutes scientific verification? In other words, might moments of genuine insight be able to ever take the place of the more reasoned approach of the scientific method which has always been part of properly investigating whatever phenomena one is observing? Furthermore, how can one be sure that their insights constitute objective reality rather than subjective experience; and where exactly does one draw the line between those two things?

That is, one can be certain during such moments of direct insight that what they have apprehended through a process of becoming fully immersed in certain aspects of their world is in fact objectively real, but still not be able to convince others of the veracity of what their moment of creative absorption has been able to teach them. Consequently, such a realization would remain incapable of expanding the frontiers of human knowledge for others simply because we have always relied on objective verification achieved through the scientific method in order for that to occur.

Yet at the same time, because the stream of our thoughts, our attention spans, and our working memories continue to be significantly dissipated by our increasingly obsessive use of digital technologies, in the future we are almost certainly going to need to depend more and more on moments of direct insight, those which might be part of a more holistic approach to intelligence, to confirm the realities of our world for us. Therefore, the question in all this would appear to be how might we objectively prove to ourselves and to others that such moments of insight do indeed carry the ring of objective truth without necessarily resorting to scientific experimentation and past knowledge as proof of this occurring?

Virginia Woolf, in her iconic, visionary novel from 1925 *Mrs. Dalloway*, explored the possibility of a consciousness that might be able to flow effortlessly between different characters, that in which their past experience, even as it might remain unconscious to both them and others, becomes part of this seemingly endless flow. It is a book, according to a recent article written for the *New York Times* by Michael Cunningham, author of the enormously successful book *The Hours*, in which the past is neither more nor less than a present which occurred in another time; a world in which, according to Cunningham, it is all but impossible to distinguish the missed opportunity from the narrow escape.

Certainly, if it is indeed possible in the real world, rather than just the world of literary imagination, for actual consciousness to pass from one person to another in a manner in which any truths embedded in that fluid consciousness can likewise be passed on with a degree of certainty about their veracity, then it might indeed be possible for moments of insight into the details of the world to be recognized as objective truth, without having to rely on a scientific veracity born of rational thought, experimentation, and previous knowledge.

However, at this point in time at least, it would appear to be difficult for objective truth to be revealed solely through a direct insight which can be passed on from the consciousness of one person to another. That is, without such truths devolving into purely subjective experience simply because the means of verification which have always been part of a scientific method that has been used to examine the veracity of conjectures about the world would be significantly missing.

Yet, as those who in the past have spent significant time examining the frontiers of consciousness have discovered, there can be truths and realities that one can be certain do indeed exist without having to subject them to the arduous process of scientific investigation based on objective, experimental verification. In fact, as those such as David Bohm have previously pointed out, the structure of our very language on which scientific exploration and verification is often based has specific limitations to which we as investigators of our world are regularly subjected.

The famous ancient Chinese philosopher Lao Tzu wrote in his iconic book *Tao Te Ching:* "the way of the heavens might be well seen without looking through a window." What he no doubt meant by these prescient words was a suggestion that truth might be observed purely and directly without literal proof or interpretation being always necessary to confirm it.

Yet at the same time, a significant question remains. Given that one may be certain of the veracity of their *aha* moment of direct insight, how might that same insight be passed on to another person vis-à-vis a moment of a shared consciousness which necessarily exists beyond the bounds of reasoned explanations and past knowledge?

In other words, if certain truths concerning various aspects of our world can indeed be apprehended purely and directly through an immediate perception, without the potential use of the scientific method to verify their existence, then it would appear to be true that the only way they might be passed on to others, who can then be certain of their veracity, is through a consciousness which flows naturally from one person to another? Yet what does that really mean, and how could it possibly occur?

As anyone who is at least somewhat familiar with the history of contemporary physics, particularly quantum physics, is already aware, scientists have begun to recognize that the universe is made of energy, rather than just being a material universe that it had been perceived as since the days of Isaac Newton. That is, quantum physicists have discovered that atoms are made of vortices of energy that are constantly spinning and vibrating.

In fact, the idea that the universe does not just consist of physical parts assembled in a certain order but comes from the entanglement of immaterial energy waves stems from the work of Albert Einstein, Max Planck, and Werner Heisenberg, among others. Therefore, since matter at its tiniest, most observable level is in fact energy, and because human consciousness is connected to such energy, scientists have speculated that that consciousness might not only be able to influence the behavior of matter but might actually be capable of restructuring it.

The famous quantum double-slit experiment is a great example of how human consciousness and our physical world might be intertwined with one another; one particular revelation of this experiment, which has been used multiple times to explore the role of consciousness in shaping reality, being that the observer creates the reality which he or she observes.

In the experiment, a double-slit optical system was used to test exactly how consciousness might affect quantum wave function; wave function in quantum physics being a mathematical description, based on probabilities, of the amplitude (or height) of quantum waves that exist in a state of isolation.

The experiment, which consists of passing a beam of light through a double-slit barrier onto a screen behind the barrier and then observing the results, was originally conducted by Thomas Young, a British physician and physicist in the late 1700s, but has been repeated numerous times by others since then with not just photons of light but also particles such as electrons, neutrons, and atoms; the results of which famous twentieth- century physicist Richard Feynman believed represents the fundamental mystery of quantum mechanics.

What has in fact been found numerous times is that when the light beam is actually observed passing through the barrier, it in fact creates a mysterious pattern of interference with itself and consequently passes through either one slit or the other. On the other hand, experimenters have found that when the beam of light is not observed passing through the barrier, it in fact is represented on a screen on the other side of the barrier as passing through both slits simultaneously.

Therefore, in a very real sense, the act of observing the light beam passing through a double-slit barrier causes it to *choose, if that word can be used, the path it will take, while not observing it creates what physicists have termed a state of superposition*, that in which the light beam in fact appears to take all possible paths simultaneously in passing through the barrier.

Therefore, relative to this experiment, and likewise relative to the subject of this book, which is how moments of direct insight might be engendered and what effects they might have, it would appear that one has to ask the question: Might it be possible for a state of heightened attention and full creative absorption, that in which the emotive, sensorial, and cognitive lives of a person are fully integrated, to not only alter the reality in which they live, but likewise be passed on to another person through a consciousness that is more fluid than what we might have previously imagined?

If these things are indeed possible, then the possibility that one might be able to change the particular reality in which one lives solely through a state of heightened attention might indeed have huge implications for many different aspects of our lives, from scientific discovery to mental health concerns to education to the search for larger metaphysical realities which might not only exist apart from the details of our everyday lives, but at the same time might even be significantly intertwined with them.

Of course, there is the question of how one might prove that such a seemingly extreme dynamic is in fact real; that it's not just the product of theoretical, otherworldly speculation. How might it be proved that a state of full creative absorption and heightened attention, one which is devoid of any further action, might not only by itself change the reality in which one lives, but likewise be passed on to another person through a consciousness that is fluid?

In order to answer these complex questions, it would appear necessary to look at the dynamic of attention and its possible effects more closely, in particular exactly what a state of heightened, focused attention entails. In doing so, likewise looking at what it means to be fully immersed in the details and dynamics of one's world to the point where that state of total immersion, by itself, actually creates change.

Quantum physicists have now demonstrated that simply observing a phenomenon, albeit one that takes place at the level of the very small, can actually change how that phenomenon occurs. So quite naturally the question now becomes one of asking if that same occurrence can take place in the details and dynamics at the macroscopic level which involve events taking place in our daily lives. That is, can a state of heightened attention and complete immersion by itself actually change how events occur?

Once again, there is the potential reality that the observer is in fact the observed; of how one actually *is* whatever one is experiencing. In the moment in which one feels jealousy, one *is* jealousy, or in looking at a beautiful tree one inwardly becomes, even if only momentarily, the beauty of that tree, just as long as one is willing to lose oneself in surrendering to a reality in which there is no psychological distance between oneself and what one is observing.

Therefore, what potential role might an *aha* moment of direct insight, that in which one's emotive, sensorial, and cognitive lives are fused as one, play in allowing a state of heightened attention by itself to effect change within the world in which one lives, and potentially within the consciousness of others?

If such is indeed the case, and it came to be accepted by cognitive scientists, neuroscientists, philosopher, educators, and others, then this development could quite possibly change a great deal, both within ourselves and likewise within a number of important institutions within our society. Particularly as far as how young people in their formative years are educated in our schools, whenever necessary more emphasis might be put on the emotive, impressionistic lives of children, even occasionally ahead of their cognitive development, so that a fully integrated intelligence might be encouraged.

Of course, cognitive development and academic learning should always be necessary components of a correct approach to educating young people, but at the same time if children are impeded from becoming fully immersed in their sensorial and emotive lives by an overemphasis on cognitive apprehension of subject matter, then an integrated intelligence often has less opportunity to flourish as those children move toward adulthood simply because those aspects of their world about which they are directing their attention soon come to be viewed, as they often are now due to force of habit, through an exclusively cognitive prism.

Chapter 11

A New Education

In the majority of our schools today there is a significant emphasis on what children learn, and how well they learn it, rather than what occurs inside them *while* they are learning. Particularly in our recently arrived digital age, that in which computer coding and algorithms are having such a profound effect on not only where people direct their attention to retrieve information, but likewise what they do next with that information, empirical validations of learning now often define not only what it means to be a successful learner, but likewise determine in advance what subject matter students learn and how they learn it.

That is to say, curricula and paths of learning which students take are becoming ever more predetermined in order to produce certain empirical results, the result of this being that students in their formative years are increasingly losing control of the paths which their learning might take due to our current emphasis on results-driven learning. Consequently, students are becoming increasingly alienated from their own experience simply because when the direction of learning paths, rather than originating within students themselves, exist outside of them in predetermined curricula, they grow inevitably separated from what their own experience might have to teach them.

At the same time, because there is now such an emphasis within the entire test-driven culture which now tends to permeate our schools and systems of education on the results of learning rather than on the process of learning itself, often resulting in an exclusively cognitive apprehension of facts and information, the emotive and sensorial lives of students are concurrently not allowed to grow as rich and fulfilling as they otherwise might become simply because they are often made to take a back seat to exclusively cognitive learning for the purpose of producing certain scores on standardized tests.

On the other hand, whenever young students in their formative years have their attention interrupted before strongly experienced impressions that have developed from their natural interests have come to full fruition, the strength of those impressions will tend to grow less vivid and powerful. It's only when those young students are permitted to follow either their emotive or their sensorial lives to a point of completion that the depth of their impressionistic lives will not be dissipated to any significant degree.

If the middle-school students who have become fascinated by some microorganisms they are apprehending by looking at them under a microscope are made to move away from that experience before they are ready to leave it in order to begin apprehending the tiny creatures only cognitively through processes like memory, classification, or linear thought, their experience, because it is impeded in this way, begins to grow shallower. Furthermore, that impeded emotive/sensorial experience, if it in fact becomes consistent and habitual, can easily become over time a self-imposed boundary on how strongly the students experience similar impressions of their world.

Of course, there is certainly a time and place for the sort of mental activities associated with important cognitive learning. However, that time and place should usually come only *after* young learners have been allowed to take their impressionistic experience with various subject matter to a point of full fruition. Otherwise, if young students are consistently compelled to move away from experiences which are strongly affecting them either emotively or sensorially, then the strength and power of those impressions may reach a certain level that by force of habit they will not be able to transcend in the future.

On the other hand, when young people are able to touch down inside the depth of their impressions, at a point where deep truths concerning certain aspects of their world begin to reveal themselves beyond the boundaries of systematic thought or previous knowledge, the possibility exists that they might be able to develop a pure, clear awareness that can often pierce to the core of things.

As anyone who is familiar with the Montessori approach to education already knows, Maria Montessori created a method for learning, particularly for children who fall into the three- to six-year age range,

which is not only highly sensorial in nature, but which attempts to facilitate a state of creative absorption in a learner by developing learning
materials which were synonymous with what she determined through
her explorations were the child's own natural interests during particular
periods of his or her development. By doing so, she endeavored to fuse
the sensorial and emotive lives of young children with their cognitive
development in a manner in which their absorption in the learning materials would engender their intelligence.

Therefore, similar to what the Montessori approach to educating
very young children attempts to engender, if our learning practices and
methods for educating children of all ages began to originate more in
the realm of the emotive and the sensorial, followed by the introduction
of cognitive learning at the correct point where it meets either or both of
these, then it would seemingly become more likely that we could begin
to facilitate an intelligence within them born of creative absorption.

What might make a genuine difference in our schools in moving
toward a correct balance of cognitive, academic learning and impressionistic apprehension of subject matter would be a new approach
to intelligence, one born of creative absorption, rather than one that
remains tightly fused with rational thought, memory, and empirical validations of how well students have been able to absorb past knowledge
that is part of predetermined curricula.

What almost certainly isn't being recognized in today's educational
climate is the effect of the increasing use of digital technologies on the
attention spans, working memories, and the potentially uninterrupted
stream of thought of those young people whose cognitive faculties
are still developing. Although this is not an issue that is now on most
people's radar screens, and in many cases is being discounted or even
completely ignored, still it needs to be significantly addressed as the
Internet age increasingly becomes our new reality, particularly for those
young people who have never known a world without it.

A jumpy, distracted awareness leading toward a diminished capacity
to attend; the overwhelming of our short-term memories to the point
where they are less able to effectively pass information to our long-term
memories; the further diminishment of our working memories due to
the use of large search engines as our brain's external hard drive where
we are actually losing touch with the very neuronal networks which
lead toward specific information and knowledge simply because we

are no longer using them to the degree which we once did. These are some of the significant negative effects which our use of the Internet and digital devices are having on all of us, particularly on young people whose cognitive lives are still developing.

However, there is another personal quality upon which our digital age may likewise be having a similarly deleterious effect. That is the potential depth of our impressions engendered by people spending so much time staring into a plastic screen in lieu of apprehending the dynamics and details of the real world, ones that exist apart from phones, PCs, and tablets, such as spending time in natural settings, where the field of one's perception and experience is greatly expanded, or by soliciting information and knowledge from real life people rather than exclusively from large search engines.

Of course, because young people in their formative years are not only using the Internet and the digital devices which connect them to it as much as adults but are likewise even more susceptible to becoming fascinated by and then addicted to the Web and digital technologies, and likewise because their impressionistic lives are still in the process of fully developing, there is an even greater danger that their inner lives will grow stifled and dulled by the potential adverse effects brought on by our current digital age of consistently apprehending virtual images on a plastic screen in lieu of real world experiences.

Consequently, as they grow toward adulthood, there is even less of a possibility that those young people's impressionistic lives will be able to grow to full fruition, thereby causing it to be less likely that future generations will be able to develop the sort of integrated, holistic intelligence alluded to in this work, that in which the depth of young people's emotive and sensorial lives will develop to the greatest degree possible.

Therefore, given that the possible deleterious effects of the Internet and the use of digital devices by young people are not about to be abrogated or diminished any time soon, one of the principal goals of an education for our present age would appear to be encouraging and strengthening the inner lives of those young people through learning activities which facilitate and allow them to stay with the depth of their impressions for longer periods of time, even occasionally in lieu of strictly cognitive approaches to subject matter; as well as creating learning activities aimed at the development of a richer emotive or sensorial life.

Academic learning for young people in their formative years, as it exists today in many schools, particularly in terms of the attempt to engender higher scores on high-stakes, standardized tests, often takes place in a highly systematic, preconceived manner in which the strength of students' impressions is significantly diluted by a singular focus on cognitive skills such as sequential thought, memorization, and classification.

Of course, there are any number of educators who will say that it is entirely possible for students to focus their attention on both significant cognitive learning and strong impressions engendered within them by that same learning. Yet those who make that argument tend to forget that it is very difficult, if not impossible, for young students to be fully involved with both types of experience, the cognitive and the impressionistic, simultaneously simply because for impressions to be experienced to the fullest possible extent, it is imperative that those young students be allowed to sink fully into them. If instead, a child is focusing solely on cognitive processes such as abstract thought, classification, sequencing, or memorization, then his capacity to become fully absorbed in his impressions is going to be significantly impeded.

In addition, although significant cognitive skills are of course important for students to develop, their facilitation often comes at the cost of teachers being able to spend more time with students assisting them in how to come more in contact with the strength of their impressions, or else setting up learning environments themselves that can allow those strongly experienced impressions to germinate.

Yet if in an age in which young people's attention spans, stream of thought, and working memories are being diminished and diluted by their incessant use of the Internet and digital devices, and there is a real need for them to develop a different type of intelligence as they move toward their adult years, one that is engendered by moments of true insight, we may well need a new type of education for students in their formative years, one in which their emotive and sensorial lives can be more effectively fused with their cognitive development as a result of their impressionistic lives being encouraged to come to full fruition.

The question of course is what type of structures for learning will allow this to occur; and how might contemporary systems and methods of learning be revamped to allow this to take place? Of course, in order to engender this new approach, the emphasis on how to educate young students is going to have to significantly change from an extreme emphasis on what specific facts and knowledge students learn and how well they learn them, as important as those things are, to what occurs inside students *while* they are learning.

As much as anything, both time and space are going to need to be permitted during classroom learning activities for students to temporarily leave academic learning to fully focus on absorbing, impressionistic experience. Whenever young people are required to consistently move away from absorbing experience before it can come to fruition, then the strength and power of impressions which they might experience at some future time may often reach only a certain level which they may not be able to transcend.

For when children in their formative years have not been able to experience certain impressions as fully as they might, then it is highly possible that the potential depth of future impressions will be filed away in their memory banks as something which can only go so far. As a result, this can easily become an intrinsic, unconscious barrier to how strongly they might experience their world as they grow toward adulthood.

Consequently, nothing might adversely affect the potential for an integrated, holistic intelligence more than a weak impressionistic life simply because without the power of strongly experienced impressions, those that are necessary to focus one's attention during moments of genuine insight, that larger intelligence might very well never be able to take place. In addition, if that weak impressionistic life begins forming during one's childhood years, then it can easily carry into adulthood, as it already has for so many adults who were educated as children vis-à-vis exclusively cognitive, results-driven approaches to learning.

On the other hand, when young people in their formative years are able to fully inhabit their impressions at a point where certain deep truths about their world begin to reveal themselves beyond the boundaries of rational thought and memory, they often begin to develop a clear, direct awareness that pierces to the heart of things. So once again, the question becomes one of how to specifically structure learning environments for young students in a manner that will properly accentuate their impressionistic lives.

The late playwright, writer, and educator George Dennison in his iconic book *The Lives of Children*, which concerned his time teaching at a progressive school situated in the Lower East Side of Manhattan during the late 1960s, that which served largely children who came from impoverished backgrounds, wrote about the idea of *losing time* while teaching school age children. The idea has to do with temporarily putting aside any proscribed, predetermined lessons in order to attend to any concerns or interests which have unexpectedly come up in students' lives, rather than squelch those in order to return to the predetermined instruction.

Consequently, if one adopts this particular approach, not only will there not be any unresolved issues negatively affecting the environment later simply because they have not been properly addressed, but when the students eventually return to the proscribed lesson, they will be able to do so without those unresolved questions or concerns impeding their attention. In addition, if one were to implement this approach to *losing time*, the capacity of students to attend would likewise be properly engendered as they grow used to not having the direction of their attention continually interrupted, as it is in many schools today as a result of adults exclusively controlling the direction of learning paths, as well as the direction of the learning environment itself.

Naturally, the next question which needs to be addressed in terms of engendering more impressionistic learning in young students would appear to be how to do so while at the same time being certain that they are acquiring the sort of skills and knowledge which they will need as they make their way toward adulthood. In other words, how might teachers and educators facilitate the development of important cognitive skills and knowledge while at the same time engendering significant impressionistic learning?

A possible answer to this question may lay in investigating two significant changes which might need to take place relative to how contemporary learning environments are now structured. The first has to do with how to keep track of student learning without employing a results-driven approach which inevitably separates students from the depth of their own experience. While the second has to do with how to properly connect students with the world of adult work so that they might acquire important skills and knowledge there rather than remaining exclusively in classroom environments which are often isolating and sterile.

Results-driven approaches to learning, those that have been significantly emboldened by current methods which often rely largely on
empirical results such as grades and test scores to track student prog-
ress, negatively affect the growth of healthy personal experience in the
learner. For when a learner is required to learn subject matter for reasons that originate entirely outside his own interests and concerns, then
his personal experience tends to become ever more separated from the
content of what he is learning simply because he is no longer in control
of the learning path by which he approaches that content. Consequently,
his personal experience tends to grow ever more dulled and disembodied; inevitably leading toward an emotive, impressionistic life that is
significantly weakened.

In addition, to manipulate students through grades and test scores
to learn particular subject matter in a predetermined manner in which
they might otherwise have no interest in becoming engaged or to make
judgments on how well they have learned subject areas, evaluations in
which the student himself has not participated, is to take the impetus
to learn something away from the student and instead replace it with a
reason for learning that invariably has little to do with the actual subject
area itself; thereby weakening the possibility that the student will be
able to in the future approach the particular area of learning with the
strength of his inner life still intact.

Therefore, the question becomes one of how to ensure that students
are acquiring significant information and knowledge in a manner in
which their impressions are emboldened, and at the same time their personal experience does not grow alienated from the content of what they
are learning. In other words, how to fuse the achievement of successful
academic learning with the growth of a rich emotive and sensorial life
so that the two might become part of the same learning process.

Because now, due to our current Internet age, knowledge and information in different subject areas is now available to students in ways in
which it has become greatly expanded and more highly complex than
it had been before, that in which there is an almost limitless number of
places toward which learning in a particular area might gravitate, there
is now a much greater opportunity to involve students in the creation of
learning progressions which might genuinely pique their interests; and
in so doing, foster the deepening of their inner lives.

In addition, because students in their formative years can now access information through the Web, rather than depend on their teachers to provide it to them, teachers now have potentially more time to work with students in developing unique, workable learning progressions in which they are genuinely interested. Consequently, the increased time that teachers now have might be well spent in assisting students in thinking creatively about how they might wish to approach different areas of learning.

Indeed, this might become a significant, if not potentially the most significant part of evaluating academic learning: how involved and successful students have become in developing their own learning progressions toward various subject matter. In addition, how successful teachers have become in involving students in creating enticing, workable learning progressions of their own might become a primary source for how they themselves are evaluated; in lieu of the test scores and various other external evaluations of learning which their students might have achieved.

Something else that might easily facilitate this process of more enriched learning would be the connection of schools and classroom environments to the world of adult work outside of school, and to working professionals who might be able to successfully pique student interest in various subject areas, provided they would be willing to spend a certain part of their workday with students in doing so.

Although the worlds of adult work and academic learning are being increasingly connected to one another, still it seems one does not hear enough in today's educational climate of regular, ongoing connections between classroom students, particularly younger students, and experts from the world of adult work. Yet at the same time, it is this movement of academic learning into the world of professional expertise outside of school that might on occasion energize young people's creative impulses and the depth of their impressions even more effectively than anything which takes place within their classroom settings.

Visiting the laboratory of a working chemist, physicist, or medical researcher; the studio of an artist; a journalist working in a busy newspaper room; the offices of a lawyer who is preparing cases or that of an investor investing money for his or her clients, and then on a regular basis, provided the working professional is willing to spend a certain amount of time with the students, work with both the professional and the students' classroom teacher to develop engaging subject matter might not only pique the students' interest in learning it, but also deepen their impressions in relation to it.

In today's hyperconnected age, the idea of the self-contained classroom, where a large number of students are taught specific subject matter by a single teacher while the students sit immobile at their desks seems entirely contrary to how the world outside of school now operates. In opposition to this now outmoded concept, giving students more control over the direction of their learning paths, and doing so in an educational climate in which they continue to be connected to adult expertise outside their classroom would not only deepen student interests and impressions relative to various subject matter, but will also prepare them more fully for the modern, hyperconnected world they will enter one day.

One way to facilitate this possible development is to tie accountability to initiative. That is, teachers might begin to determine student accountability largely by assessing how involved students have become in creating their own learning progressions in acquiring knowledge and information associated with various subject matter.

In short, is there a way to fuse initiative with accountability so that students, even at a very young age, with of course the requisite amount of assistance from adults, are held more accountable for developing the initiative to explore the acquisition of certain subject matter and skills in creative ways that genuinely interest them? While, at the same time, are held less accountable for meeting predetermined, adult conceived standards of learning that the students have not only had no real hand in creating, but likewise have little or no understanding of in terms of how these specifically relate to the content of what they are learning.

There is in fact no better way to create dulled, disembodied experience in young learners than to separate standards of accountability for learning from the initiative of students to learn various subject matter simply because they have a specific interest in doing so. When that occurs, students are in a very real sense outside their own experience simply because the path toward which they are acquiring various information and knowledge, that which they are required to follow if they are to be deemed successful learners, has now become something that is now exterior to their own interests and strongly experienced impressions.

Therefore, if one of the goals of our current education system is to foster the sort of integrated intelligence which has been the subject of this book, one which is significantly based on the development of a healthy, enriching emotive and sensorial life, then it seems imperative that schools and classrooms begin to fuse accountability with initiative, rather than continue to subject students to standards of accountability for learning that are essentially exterior to their own inner lives.

Involving students in the development of their own learning progressions causes students to grow connected to areas of learning as a whole, rather than causing them to become familiar with subject matter in a more restrictive manner in which only isolated pieces of information are connected to one another. On the other hand, when young people are permitted and encouraged to create their own path toward knowledge and information which they are assimilating, their understanding of the entire subject matter becomes more complete, and in the process their emotive lives and impressions centering on the particular area of learning grow ever more vivid.

However, if this more process-oriented approach to learning in which students create their own learning progressions toward various subject matter is to come to fruition in our schools, then both the structure and purpose of contemporary classrooms is going to have to change in order to allow this to occur.

In short, the impressionistic lives of young learners are going to need to be permitted to find a place at the center of modern classrooms, whether those classrooms exist in either private or public schools. In conjunction with this, opportunities for learning can be engendered which parallel the sort of creative, collaborative thinking that has become a hallmark for success in the world of adult work. Consequently, a truer, more complete initiative to learn might be engendered in students, one that simultaneously enriches not just their cognitive but likewise their emotive and sensorial lives on the way toward the potential growth in them of a more holistic, integrated intelligence.

Chapter 12

A Larger Intelligence

As has been elucidated in this work, because many people's attention spans and the stream of their thoughts are being continually fragmented and interrupted by the way the Internet operates and by their continuous use of digital devices; because we are often outsourcing our working memories to large search engines, and in so doing short-circuiting the neuronal pathways inside our brains which lead toward specific information and knowledge; and because the potential depth of our emotive lives and the sharpness of our impressions are often being dulled by our continuous acquaintance with artificial images on a plastic screen in lieu of observations of and experience with the fabric of life which takes place in the real world, the development of our intelligence is being significantly impeded.

In order to adapt to the impact of these influences of our current digital world on our thoughts, memories, and emotive lives, it may be necessary for us to view what intelligent thought and behavior mean through a fundamentally different lens; one in which the capacity for direct insight and creative absorption might to a certain extent begin to take the place of rational thought and the knowledge apprehended by our working memories as primary ingredients.

In order to have a moment of direct insight into the details and dynamics of the world in which one lives, it is imperative that that insight occur at a place which significantly challenges one's previous understanding of whatever one is observing. Otherwise, that previous understanding, particularly if it occurs at only the cognitive level, can easily serve as a barrier to a new moment of insight simply because moments of direct insight must necessarily be anchored in a present that is entirely free from the suppositions and knowledge of the past.

Yet at the same time, our thoughts tend to exist in the past, a product of our past experiences being projected into the future. Because of this constant movement from past to future, it often becomes impossible for us to live entirely within the present moment. Therefore, because we are continually carrying with us thoughts concerning our past experiences, those thoughts and remembrances can easily block moments of true insight from occurring, those which by their very nature must be free from the weight of past experience.

In addition, because a flow state, discussed earlier as one that is synonymous with moments of direct insight, often carries with it a loss of self-consciousness and a distortion of time, one in which the movement of time itself veritably seems to disappear as one becomes thoroughly immersed in the present moment, the pendulum of thought swinging incessantly between past and future is almost certainly a significant impediment to achieving moments of insight and absorption.

Yet because it can be so difficult to live thoroughly in the present moment, in that space between two thoughts, we are often kept from becoming thoroughly immersed in the details and dynamics of the world in which we live; part of the problem simply being that our cognitive, emotive, and sensorial lives tend to be so compartmentalized that they are essentially kept separate from one another. Consequently, the present moment, which often contains significant elements of emotive and sensorial experience, is unable to come fully alive in a moment of immediate absorption and insight in which one's impressionistic life is fundamentally enriched.

As long as human intelligence continues to be viewed as an essentially cognitive activity in which the quality of one's thoughts and past knowledge is what primarily allows one to successfully negotiate his or her world, our observations of and interactions with that world may well continue to be limited by this cognitive barrier, and as a result we will continue to view our world less impressionistically and likewise less completely.

Yet how might one observe one's world clearly and respond to it appropriately without using conceptual thought, memory, and the knowledge which one has attained through past experiences as one's guide? In other words, is there a way to use thought when it is needed to see one's world clearly and thus react to it appropriately, and at the same time dispense with thought when it becomes an impediment to the attainment of a more inclusive holistic intelligence?

Whenever thought begins to define either our emotive or our sensorial reactions to occurrences in our lives, it tends to limit what those reactions might become. That is, the definition is what often causes us to experience our impressions of the world according to how we have defined them to ourselves in advance. By naming and defining those impressions, there is a tendency to stop pursuing them further whenever that which we are experiencing is in conflict with the name or definition which we have attributed to it.

Therefore, the question would appear to be: Can we fully experience our impressions, feelings, or sensorial reactions without comprehending them cognitively? Or are the definition and names which our thoughts give to our impressions of the world necessary for us to have a full and complete understanding of those impressions?

The amygdala is the region of the brain that is concerned with emotions. In doing so, it coordinates responses in the brain in connection with emotional states, and it is what underlies emotional memory. It likewise connects with other regions of the brain which process conscious awareness of our bodily responses, with structures that are responsible for cognition, such as the prefrontal cortex, and with those pathways which are responsible for perception of objects. In facilitating these and other processes, the amygdala can communicate with nearly every region of the brain that is responsible for emotional reactions.

Elizabeth Phelps, Professor of Human Neuroscience at Harvard University, known for her research at the intersection of memory, learning, and emotion, has proposed that the primary work of the amygdala involves coordinating the response of neural circuits in the brain to emotional cues; switching certain circuits on and off when an emotion is either appropriate or inappropriate relative to the various potential responses to a particular situation.

Relative to how the amygdala region of the brain so thoroughly connects emotional responses and cues to cognitive structures which produce our thoughts, it seems that it might indeed be worthwhile to ask not only how habitual these connections can become, and likewise how amenable they might be to change through disciplined mental activity, such as that which occurs for example, during mindfulness training. In addition, another question which seems as if it might need to be explored is if certain connections between thought and emotions might be somehow impeded so that an individual can on occasion experience the purity of his or her emotive life free from the interference of thought or memory.

Obviously, what has become a habitual part of our awareness of our feelings and sensorial reactions is the idea that we need to first name and classify these so that we can better understand them. That is, if we can't name or define envy, fear, hate, love, joy, or sympathy, then how can we possibly deal with these as significant parts of our lives? At least that has traditionally been our thinking as far as the necessity of first understanding with our thoughts and memories what we are feeling or experiencing emotively or sensorially in order to use those dynamics to act intelligently.

Therefore, the question becomes one of asking if the comprehension of our feelings and physical reactions to the world can indeed potentially take place without understanding them through thought and memory. In other words, can there potentially be a moment of direct insight which allows us to understand certain situations or facets of our world without having to put that moment of insight into thoughts or words; in the process allowing the insight to remain truer and more powerful simply because we are not attempting to limit it by defining or categorizing it.

As many who came of age during the period of the 1970s might remember, researcher and author Carlos Castaneda wrote his series of books in which the Yaqui Indian Don Juan took Castaneda under his tutelage for the purpose of helping him become what he referred to as *a man of knowledge*; Don Juan speaking often of the need to shrink the creations of the self, those that have traditionally been part of our two-dimensional reality, one engendered by the world of our thoughts, in order to approach the world of a limitless awareness existing beyond the intrinsic barriers of thought and memory, one which he tells Castaneda can only be approached through intuitive, direct insight.

Krishnamurti spoke often of a state of choiceless awareness in which one understands immediately what action he or she needs to take in a particular situation without having to make a conscious decision simply by seeing the particular situation purely and directly beyond the bounds of rational decision making and memories of past experiences, and then acting solely from that awareness. It is a place where direct insight and intelligent action become one and the same.

In his classic book *The Wisdom of Insecurity,* Alan Watts wrote about how we are forever impeding what he called *the stream of life,* that endless flow of events in our lives, by not simply allowing those events and occurrences to flow ceaselessly forward into one another through a reliance on fixed concepts generated by our thoughts and memories, those by which we hope to understand our experiences. In doing so, we may not be allowing ourselves to potentially comprehend the interconnectivity of those experiences as part of a larger reality.

If it is indeed possible to fully integrate our cognitive, emotive, and sensorial lives for the purpose of engendering moments of insight, our daily experiences might likewise become more meaningful as they integrate more fully with one another. That is, we may be able to see just how fully one moment in our lives leads into and influences the next, even those that we might have tended to apprehend as emanating from different parts of our existence. In so doing, we may be able to gain a greater perspective on our own life and on the lives of others with whom we interact.

Writers like Marcel Proust, James Joyce, Virginia Woolf, Henry Miller, and Jack Kerouac have all explored the incessant forward movement of consciousness, one which we ourselves might apprehend provided we are alive to it; particularly in the case of Woolf even allowing that consciousness to jump back and forth fluidly between different characters who are part of a similar storyline or setting. In our own lives, however, what often prevents us from experiencing Watts's *stream of life*, one in which we allow one momentary experience to not only flow into but even significantly affect the next, is the continual definition, naming, and classification of our experiences through the use of thought, knowledge, and memory.

In Arthur Miller's iconic play *Death of a Salesman,* Miller's tragic character Willie Lohman is an aging salesman who toward the end of his life experiences his dream of a better life for himself and his older son Biff going up in smoke. Yet at the same time because he is so determined to hang onto and live in a world that was never really there, he ends up destroying both himself and his family as an illusory world of success that he has created for both himself and his family comes crashing into the hard barrier of real-life experience.

Without growing too metaphorical, so many of our own lives are like Willie's, even if not to the extreme that determined his own tragic outcome. That is, because we so continually define for ourselves what we are experiencing in the moment, rather than allowing ourselves to experience it purely and directly without the barriers of thought, memory, and past knowledge to cloud our perceptions, we often remain one step removed from what we are actually experiencing.

R.D. Laing, the famous radical psychotherapist from the 1960s, wrote in his influential book *The Politics of Experience* that just as we are taught by our fellow human beings what behavior is appropriate and what is not in interpersonal situations, we are likewise taught by others what to experience and what not to experience from an entire range of possible experiences. Laing then goes on to describe how so often our experience can become essentially mystified and unreal for us when others provide us with false descriptions of what is occurring within ourselves.

Whether or not one tends to agree with Laing's description of how our experience can essentially become politicized in this way, still it is almost certainly the naming, defining, and labeling of experiences in our life in the moment in which they are occurring which can so easily create a false narrative within us of what we are experiencing. Yet how do we comprehend our own experience without employing our thoughts and working memory to understand it, and in so doing limiting what it might become? That would appear to be the important question here.

In short, is there a moment of direct insight in which we can fully comprehend whatever we are experiencing without attempting to either name it, explain it to ourselves, or compare it to past experiences we might have had? And if so, could that moment of insight actually be part of a larger intelligence?

None of our emotions or sensorial reactions ever occur in isolation. They are all part of the web of interrelationships which each of us has with the world in which we live. Jealousy of a particular person always emanates from the nature of the relationship which one has with that person. Likewise, our reaction to a beautiful piece of music or painting always occurs within the context of the depth of appreciation which one has previously developed for certain types of art.

Therefore, if our feelings and sensorial reactions always occur within the context of the particular relationship we have with our outer environment, it seems possible that rather than naming or defining those emotions or physical reactions in order to understand exactly what they are, we can instead apprehend them clearly by simply observing what their relationship is to occurrences in our lives.

For example, we don't need to name, describe, or analyze a feeling of jealousy that has begun to germinate within us in order to fully experience it. If we are paying close attention to how we react to other people, we can see jealousy clearly for what it is without limiting the feeling by naming or analyzing it, and in so doing attempting to push it back down inside ourselves in a neurotic fashion. Rather, by simply recognizing it in how we react to others, and then allowing the feeling of jealousy to grow to full fruition at a place that exists on the other side of thought and memory, it can potentially begin to dissipate and dissolve.

Likewise, in listening to a beautiful piece of classical music, one doesn't need to name or define for themselves what they are feeling in order to fully experience the particular emotion or physical sensation that has just taken place within them. In fact, in doing so they will only tend to limit those things vis-à-vis their thoughts and memories. Rather, if they simply allow themselves to become completely absorbed in what they are listening to, they will most likely have understood its full effect upon them without having to name, label, or even think about what they have just heard.

There is almost certainly an intelligence that is innately part of our emotive and sensorial reactions to events in our lives, and if we can use our thoughts to clarify those reactions only after we have allowed our feelings and physical reactions to grow to full fruition, our intelligence might then become more complete and more whole. Once again, the development of such a holistic intelligence might indeed be necessary amidst a digital age in which the stream of our thoughts and our attention spans are being continually impeded, and our working memories are being constantly diluted due to the effects of the Internet, and by how people are compulsively using their digital devices.

Traditionally, thoughts, feelings, and sensorial reactions have often been put into separate boxes, rather than seen as things which profoundly influence one another. Yet if we are to explore the possibility of a larger intelligence, particularly in the midst of our current Internet age, it seems imperative that we begin to explore more fully the effects of thought and memory on our impressionistic lives; particularly for those people who have an intense curiosity to explore the possibility of a consciousness that reaches toward a limitless reality which might exist at a place beyond thought and memory.

With the introduction of quantum theory, physical science has explored the effects of human behavior and the physical world on each other in the search for a larger view of physical reality. Now it seems time for the worlds of psychology, education, and behavioral science to fully explore the effects of our cognitive, emotive, and sensorial lives on each other in the search for a larger intelligence.

Unfortunately, the one thing that tends to stand in the way of this occurring are predetermined views and approaches to our emotive/sensorial life which tend to define and categorize what is taking place within us; a tendency which might often need to be left alone so that we might be able to view our interior life more clearly by allowing occurrences there to reach a point of full fruition before we attempt to understand them.

A key to allowing this to occur would almost certainly be a concise realization concerning the limitations of our thinking minds; when our thoughts might serve to clarify our day-to-day reality for us, and when they impede it by dulling our impressions of the world in which we live. Ultimately, the richer our emotive and sensorial lives are, the sharper our perceptions of our world become.

For anyone seeking a larger, more expansive intelligence which might exist beyond the boundaries of thought and memory, one which might on occasion begin to approach a consciousness which touches upon an apprehension of a limitless world in which one's interior world and outer environment become one, the integration of our perceptions, emotions, and sensorial reactions into a larger awareness would appear to be not only important, but even critically necessary.

One place where this potential path of discovery might begin is through a more complete integration of the areas of the metaphysical, psychological, scientific, and educational into one another for the purposes of allowing the search for a larger intelligence to become a significant part of all these different fields of inquiry.

For to limit metaphysical concerns to proscribed steps and practices leading toward a larger awareness, rather than an exploration into the barriers of the self; to limit therapeutic practices in the field of psychology to only helping someone better adapt to his/her world, rather than as an exploration by therapist and patient alike (if one wants to use those terms) working to enlighten each other in regard to a larger consciousness which might exist beyond the self; to put boundaries between physical scientists exploring the physical and biological universe and the exploration of a larger consciousness; or to limit the education of students in their formative years to the successful acquisition of knowledge and facts, rather than focusing more importantly on what is taking place *inside* those students while that acquisition is taking place is to in effect limit all those fields of endeavor in unhealthy ways.

The appearance of the Internet and other technologies which people use to communicate with each other more easily in our current digital age has no doubt brought many significant positive developments to our modern world, those which have made all our lives exponentially easier in any number of ways. Yet if the digital world is also impeding the stream of our thoughts, narrowing our attention spans, and stifling our working memories, for which there is increasing evidence that all of these potentially negative developments are indeed occurring, then the Web and people's habitual use of digital devices is likewise negatively affecting our overall level of intelligence, causing it to become shallower and more constricted.

Therefore, in response to this potentially menacing development we may well need to both recognize and develop a new type of intelligence, one which is not so reliant upon two-dimensional thought processes and a working memory that originates with past experience; and instead embrace the power of impressionistic absorption into the details and dynamics of our world, thus allowing it to begin replacing rational thought and past knowledge as cornerstones of this new intelligence.

The Internet and digital world have now become, for better or for worse, the new reality in which we live. We can either ignore its implications for our mental, emotive, and sensorial lives or we as humans can seek a new type of awareness, one which fuses the different aspects of our inner domain. In so doing we might begin to look at our world with fresh eyes, ones in which our evolutionary journey as creative beings can no longer be adversely affected in circular fashion by the new technologies which we have created.

Then, as part of that same journey, we might begin to explore the possibility of a world that is no longer limited by the barriers of rational thought, the past, and memory; one in which our inner and outer worlds become absorbed into one another as we grow more complete in our personal development; one in which intuitive understanding can occur inside the world of an intelligence which reaches toward a limitless apprehension of ourselves and our world; and one in which we are more directly in touch with what we are actually experiencing from moment to moment in our daily lives.

Bibliography

Aczel, Amir D. *Entanglement.* New York: Plume, a member of Penguin Group (USA) Inc., 2001.

Apex Brain Centers. *3 Real Life Examples of Brain Plasticity.* Apexbraincenters. com, May, 2014.

Armstrong, Kim. *Interoception: How We Understand Our Body's Inner Sensations. Association for Psychological Science*, October, 2019.

Bargh, John. *Embodied Cognition: Definition, Theory & Experiments.* Study. com.

Bekoff, Mark. *The Emotional Lives of Animals.*

Benson, Etienne. *Intelligence across Cultures. American Psychological Association*, February, 2003, Vol. 34, No. 2.

Biography Online, *Beethoven Biography.*

Boeree, George C. *Personality Theory: A Biosocial Approach.* webspace. ship.edu, 2009.

Bohm, David. *Wholeness and the Implicate Order.* London: Routledge, 1980.

Brown, Allison. *Change Your Feelings by First Changing Your Thoughts.* Family Therapy.

Cannon, W. B. *Bodily Changes in Pain, Hunger, Fear, and Rage: An Account of Recent Researches into the Function of Emotional Excitement.* New York: D. Appleton & Co., 1915.

Carr, Nicholas. *The Shallows: What the Internet Is Doing to Our Brains.* New York: W. W. Norton, 2011, 2010.

Castaneda, Carlos. *Tales of Power.* New York: Simon and Schuster, 1974.

Center of Bethesda, February 5, 2019. *The Emotional Lives of Animals. Yes! Magazine*, January 17, 2019.

The Chicago School of Professional Psychology. *What Is Native Intelligence?* October 26, 2016.

Csikszentmihalyi, Mihaly. *Creativity: Flow and the Psychology of Discovery and Invention.* New York: HarperCollins, 1996.

Cunningham, Michael. *Michael Cunningham on Virginia Woolf's Literary Revolution. The New York Times*, December 23, 2020.

Dennison, George. *The Lives of Children.* Reading, MA: Addison-Wesley Publishing Company, Inc., 1969.

Dewey, John. *The School and Society.* Chicago: University of Chicago Press, 1899. *The Child and the Curriculum.* London: The University of Chicago Press, 1902.

Dubois, Julien, Paola Galdi, Lynn K. Paul, and Ralph Adolphs. *A Distributed Brain Network Predicts General Intelligence from Resting-State Human Neuroimaging Data.* Royal Society Publishing, August 13, 2018.

Fradera, Alex. New Cross-Cultural Analysis Suggests that g or "general intelligence" Is a Human Universal. *Research Digest*, April 24, 2018.

Frey, Joyce. *A Toroidal Representation of Intelligence from a Plains Cree Lens: A Bridge Toward Enlightenment. Fourth World Journal* (CWIS) Summer, 2017. Vol. 16 #1.

Frijda, N. H. 2005. *Emotion, Experience, Cognition and Attention 19:* 473–498.

Gardner, Howard. *Frames of Mind: The Theory of Multiple Intelligences.* New York: Basic Books, 1983.

Georgia State University. *New Insight into Brain Connectivity. Science Daily*, January 23, 2020.

Gold, Joshua, and Joseph Ciociari. *A Transactional Stimulation Intention to Support Flow State Induction. frontiers in Human Neuroscience*, August 8, 2019.

Goleman, Daniel. *Emotional Intelligence.* New York: Bantam Books, 1995.

Gray, K., S. Anderson, E. E. Chen, J. M. Kelly, M. S. Christian, J. Patrick, L. Huang, T. N. Kenett, and K. Lewis. Forward Flow: A New Measure to Quantify Free Thought and Predict Creativity. *American Psychologist*, 2019.

Greenfield, Susan. *Mind Change: How Digital Technologies Are Leaving Their Marks on Our Brain.* New York: Random House, 2015.

Gregory, Richard L. *Eye and Brain: The Psychology of Seeing.* New York: Oxford University Press, 1998.

Hoffman, Leon, M.D. *Emotions Affect Cognitions. Psychology Today*, October 23, 2011.

Huxley, Aldous. *The Doors of Perception.* New York: HarperCollins, 1954.

Illich, Ivan. *Deschooling Society.* London: Marion Bogars, 1970.

Isaacson, Walter. *Einstein: His Life and Universe.* New York: Simon and Schuster, 2007.

James, William, 1884. *What Is an Emotion? Mind 9*: 188–205.

Johns Hopkins Medicine. *Inside the Science of Memory.* www.hopkinsmedi-cine.org, 2020.

Jung, Carl. *Collected Works of C.G. Jung. Volume 9 (Part 1): Archetypes and the Collective Unconscious.* Princeton, NJ: Princeton University Press, 1st ed., 1969.

Kandel, Eric. *In Search of Memory.* New York: W.W. Norton, 2006. *The Age of Insight: The Quest to Understand the Unconscious in Art, Mind, and Brain.* New York: Random House, 2012.

Kounios, John and Mark Jung-Beeman. *The Aha Moment: The Cognitive Neuroscience of Insight. APS: A Journal of the Association for Psychological Science* (2009).

Krishnamurti, J. *The Awakening of Intelligence.* New York: HarperCollins, 1973. *The Wholeness of Life.* New York: Harper and Row, 1979.

Laing, R. D. *The Politics of Experience.* New York: Pantheon Books, 1967.

Lewis, Ralph, M.D. What Actually Is a Thought? And How Is Information Physical? *Psychology Today*, February 24, 2019.

Lewis, Tanya. *Connectivity Is Key to Understanding the Brain. Live Science*, October 31, 2013.

Macedonia, Manuela. *Embodied Learning: Why at School the Mind Needs the Body. frontiers in Psychology*, October 1, 2019.

Mahler, Kelly. *What Is Interoception?* www.kelly-mahler.com, 2020.

Marenus, Michele. *Gardner's Theory of Multiple Intelligences. Simply Psychology*, June 9, 2020.

McKinnon, Amy. *A Melding of Humanities, Sciences. Harvard Gazette*, March 3, 2018.

Miller, Arthur I. *Einstein, Picasso: Space, Time, and the Beauty That Causes Havoc.* New York: Basic Books, 2001.

Montessori, Maria. *The Absorbent Mind.* New York: Holt, Rinehart, and Winston, Inc., 1967.

Nakamura, Jeanne, and Mihaly Csikszentmihalyi. *Flow Theory and Research.* Oxford Handbook of Positive Psychology, 2009.

Neuroscience News. *How Emotions Are Mapped in the Brain.* https://neurosci-encenews.com, January 24, 2020.

Nitsch, Twylah. *Entering into the Silence: The Seneca Way.* The Seneca Indian Historical Society, 1976.

Oosterwijk Suzanne, Kristen Lindquist, Eric Anderson, Rebecca Dantoff, Yoshiga Moriguchi, and Lisa Feldman Barrett. *States of Mind: Emotions, Body Feelings, and Thoughts Share Distributed Neural Networks.* HHS Public Access, June 5, 2012.

Oppland, Mike. *8 Ways to Create Flow According to Mihaly Csikszentmihalyi. Positive Psychology*, December 10, 2020.

Piaget, Jean and Barbel Inhelder. *The Psychology of the Child.* Translated by Helen Weaver. New York: Basic Books, 1969.

Pulvermiller, F. *Brain Mechanisms Linking Language and Action. Nature Reviews Neuroscience* 6 (2005) (7): 576–582.

Schacter S., and J. E. Singer. *Cognitive, Social, and Physiological Determinants of Emotional States. Psychological Review* 69: 379–399.

Shearer, C. B. *A Resting State Functional Connectivity Analysis of Human Intelligence: Broad Theoretical and Practical Implications for Multiple Intelligences Theory. APA PsycNet,* 2020.

Sheldrake, Rupert. *A New Science of Life: The Hypothesis of Formative Causation.* Los Angeles, CA: J.P. Tarcher, 1981. *Morphic Resonance and Morphic Fields—an Introduction.* www.sheldrake.org.

sixseconds; The Emotional Intelligence Network. *Integrated Emotions: Rethinking feelings as allies so we can escape the negative emotions' trap. August 17,* 2020.

Sperber, Michael and Brent Ranalli. *Thoreau's PTSD and Posttraumatic Growth. Thoreau Society Bulletin.* Fall, 2020.

Stanford Encyclopedia of Philosophy. *Embodied Cognition.* July 25, 2011.

Sullivan, J.W.N. *Beethoven: His Spiritual Development.* Read & Co. Books, 2020.

Sullivan, Robert. *The Thoreau You Don't Know.* New York: HarperCollins, 2009.

Thoreau, Henry David. *Walden; Or Life in the Woods.* Boston: Ticknor and Fields, 1854.

Tucker, Lacey. *Connections between Neuroscience and the Theory of Multiple Intelligences; Implications for Education.* Serendip, 1999 Third Web Reports.

Varela, Francisco J., Evan Thompson, and Eleanor Rosch. *The Embodied Mind: Cognitive Science and Human Experience. MIT Press.* November 13, 1992.

Vinney, Cynthis. *What Is a Flow State in Psychology? Thought Co.,* Updated December 12, 2019.

Walia, Arjun. *Science Proves That Human Consciousness and Our Material World Are Intertwined: See For Yourself. Collective Evolution,* March 8, 2014.

Watts, Alan W. *The Wisdom of Insecurity.* New York: Pantheon Books, 1951.

Woods, Alan. *Beethoven: Man, Composer, and Revolutionary.* www.marxist. com., December 17, 2020.

Woolf, Virginia. *Mrs. Dalloway.* London: Harcourt, Inc., 1925.

World Psychiatry. *The Online Brain: How the Internet May Be Changing Our Cognition.* 2019 June, 18 (2): 119–129.

Ye Liu, Qiufang Fu, and Xiaolan Fu. *The Interaction Between Cognition and Emotion. Research Gate,* November, 2009.

Index

ability: of animals, 59; cognitive, 1, 16, 69; to focus, 8, 79
absorbing experience, in education, 100
absorption, creative, 5, 10, 17, 29, 32; artwork and, 34; cognitive mind and, 80; complexity of creative task and, 42; education and, 97
abstract thought, 85
acceptance, of emotions, 21, 46, 68–69, 113
accommodation, of new information, 47
accountability, of students, 104–5
activity, cognitive, 108
Adaptation (film), 25–27
addiction, to Internet: as physiological or psychological, 7
Against Interpretation (Sontag), 83
age, Internet, ix, xiii, xiv, 98, 102, 115
The Age of Insight (Kandel), 9, 31
aha moment, 31, 34, 68, 92
amygdala, in brain, 109

animals: ability of, 59; emotions of, 59–61
archetypes, of Jung, 60
artist, concert hall and, 32–34
artistic output, challenging emotional experience and, 77
artwork, creative absorption and, 34
assimilation, of new information, 47
atoms, energy and, 90
attention: concentration contrasted with, 78–79; internet and span of, 2, 8, 12, 14; selective, 25–26
awareness: distracted, 52; enhanced, ix–x, xiv, xv, 13, 79

Barrett, Lisa Feldman, 71–72
Beethoven, Ludwig van, 76–77, 78, 82
Bekoff, Mark, 59
Biff (fictional character, *Death of a Salesman*), 111
Bohm, David, 10–11, 66–67, 89
brain: amygdala region of, 109; cerebral cortex of, 81; core task of, 72; hippocampus region of, 23, 57; plasticity of, 44, 52–53;

About the Author

For twelve years, **Lyn Lesch** was founder and director of The Children's School in Evanston, Illinois, a private, progressive, democratically run school for children six to fourteen years of age. During its existence, the school received widespread attention in both electronic and print media in the Chicago area as a unique, innovative approach to education.

He is also the author of four books on education reform, all of them stressing the importance of what occurs inside children *while* they learn, as opposed to results-driven approaches.

In 2020 he wrote and published *Intelligence in the Digital Age: How the Search for Something Larger May Be Imperiled*, a book which concerns how our current Internet age and people's use of digital technologies may be affecting their mental capacities and emotive lives in ways that will make it increasingly difficult for those who choose to do so to explore a larger, more expansive consciousness.

Lyn can be found at his author website *lynlesch.com,* writing and blogging about this search for a larger, more enriched intelligence, particularly in terms of the effects that modern technology in our current Internet age may be having upon it.

About the Author

*9 7 8 1 4 7 5 8 6 3 7 4 1 *